D1805958

Seeing
Eye to Eye

Seeing
Eye to Eye

How people professionals can achieve lasting
alignment and success within their business

JONATHAN KETTLEBOROUGH

authorHOUSE®

AuthorHouse™
1663 Liberty Drive
Bloomington, IN 47403
www.authorhouse.com
Phone: 1-800-839-8640

© 2012 by Jonathan Kettleborough. All rights reserved.

No part of this book may be reproduced, stored in a retrieval system, or transmitted by any means without the written permission of the author.

Published by AuthorHouse   11/28/2012

ISBN: 978-1-4772-4673-3 (sc)
ISBN: 978-1-4772-4674-0 (hc)
ISBN: 978-1-4772-4676-4 (e)

Any people depicted in stock imagery provided by Thinkstock are models, and such images are being used for illustrative purposes only.
Certain stock imagery © Thinkstock.

Because of the dynamic nature of the Internet, any web addresses or links contained in this book may have changed since publication and may no longer be valid. The views expressed in this work are solely those of the author and do not necessarily reflect the views of the publisher, and the publisher hereby disclaims any responsibility for them.

To Mum, for always showing me the power of perseverance over mediocrity.

To Dad, for showing me patience and common sense.

To Joe and Will, because all things are possible, even though some take a little longer.

"Writing a book is an adventure. To begin with it is a toy and an amusement. Then it becomes a mistress, then it becomes a master, then it becomes a tyrant. The last phase is that just as you are about to be reconciled to your servitude, you kill the monster and fling him to the public."

Winston Churchill

CONTENTS

FOREWORD

It's always a great honour to be asked to write a foreword, even more so when it's about something you passionately, fervently and intellectually agree with. When discussing this book with Jonathan, I got more passionate, fervent and then intellectually grasped by what he had to say.

My view is that as a profession, we've come on in leaps and bounds in terms of recognition of the impact we have; yet still we often find ourselves in an inferior position to our colleagues in Finance, Legal, IT, Marketing, and Research & Development. In a world where service and product differentiation is driven increasingly by the people in organisations, that is simply no longer acceptable.

Therefore I am delighted to endorse Jonathan's work and words in this book as he has hit on one of the key things which will enable our profession to "muscle in" on the equation of business success—ALIGNMENT. Quite simply put, we need to be aligned in everything we do:

- Align rewards mechanics to performance and results in a way that is not just about appraisal markings for output but more about behaviours, social connectivity, innovation and of course, as I said earlier, service differentiation.
- Align our attraction and on-board mechanics to those that make the business accelerate, not stutter. If people are the fuel of the organisation's engine, we need new people to be an additive, not a temporary drag. The way we induct, develop and unleash new talent should be our greatest gift to a business, but instead it is often our greatest detracting factor.
- Align our employment frames and references. Call them policies, if you will, but policies become policing, which rarely enables brilliance—rather they serve as catch-all rules for misdemeanours and regulations and can erode trust as much as build protection. We need to be able to act as a mutual organisation—like the John Lewis Partnership: we will give you freedom, ownership rights and a voice, and the trade-off is you act professionally, responsibly and with inventiveness that moves our business forward.

Most of all we need to find people the right place for the talents they have so they can develop and unleash their potential. This is the ultimate in alignment. Get people in the right role, where they thrive, share and drive, and we—as shareholders, consumers, colleagues and managers—all benefit.

I won't use this foreword to batter managers any more than they already are. Certainly, as the lid is lifted on complicit practices, corrupt actions and bonus-driven strategies that serve themselves over all others, trust in senior leaders is at an all-time low. What we DO need in our industry is backing, belief and collaboration from our managers in the field. We have had a tricky relationship with managers. We don't always serve them well, and even when we do, we can adopt a slightly "stone-throwing" approach and criticise them for the organisation's failings. Our profession is in a glass house and therefore we need to be more collaborative with our managers, who in turn should deliver a better people-proposition in the workplace.

With remote working on the rise, flexible patterns, expertise droughts and the need for market-leading innovation from the bottom up, more than ever our time is now. Alignment is the key that unlocks that door. Without alignment of case, purpose, impact, relevance, feasibility and sustainability, it will simply fall at one or more of those hurdles.

I am therefore delighted to be asked to put something provocative into Jonathan's book and set out my own thoughts on why this book is so badly needed, right now, for us ALL in our profession.

So what has Jonathan given us with this book?

Firstly, the benefit of his experience and insight; without being a spoiler for the rest of the book, it is littered with examples of real improvements made in real places with genuine impact.

Secondly, Jonathan reminds us of why we are in this game, and why we need to act, operate and deliver in certain ways, in certain areas and with a huge dollop of context, reality and purpose.

Thirdly, and most importantly for me, Jonathan sets out a call to action. We all know we need more clout; we need more influence and we need to be involved in pioneering activities which get the best from people in organisations. Sadly we talk about it a lot like this, as it's not an omnipresent feature for us. I doubt accountants have the same conversations as we do about being heard. This call to action is why this is a "right now" book—a book with the back story based on insight; the relevance and contextual frames that link up ALL parts of our profession; and then the prod to get a little more bravery, guile and creativity around the way we do business.

So with that in mind, I will leave you to make the most of this interesting, impact-led, encouraging thinking from Jonathan and I hope the next foreword I write is about how we capitalise on our new-found position of influence and push on even further.

Alignment is perhaps the new key skill that brings our profession—once and for all—out of the black holes and into the white spaces of business. Well done, Jonathan, for bringing that to the front of our minds. We're aligned with you all the way.

Perry Timms
Director—PTHR
People and Transformational HR

INTRODUCTION

"Whenever you see a successful business, someone once made a courageous decision."

Peter Drucker

Austrian-born American management consultant, educator, and author, whose writings contributed to the philosophical and practical foundations of the modern business corporation.

The challenge

The People Professional is under pressure from all areas. They are being asked to deliver more with less, to justify their existence and to show how their activities have a positive benefit on the businesses they serve. Budgets are constantly under pressure and in some quarters are being slashed. Times are tight and are set to stay that way for some time to come.

It doesn't have to be this way. It's possible to rise above these issues and really demonstrate what that People Profession can deliver, but to do that we must listen first and foremost to the needs of our businesses, for if we do that, and do it right, we can set ourselves up for long-term success. It's our future and it's in our hands.

Welcome

Many books that are written for People Professionals are aimed at telling you how to develop or deliver training or how to coach or mentor or how to recruit staff or any of the many things that People Professionals deal with on an everyday basis. This book is different.

This book comes with a clear health warning: it will not cure all known ills, nor is it the source of all knowledge, and it will certainly not solve all your problems! What it will do is point you in the right direction for all your people efforts, ensuring that you place your efforts and resources in the right place at the right time in order to fix the right problems. It will also change the way that the people business is viewed in your organisation but only if you work at it.

Overview of the book

The book has twelve chapters, each dealing with a specific area of alignment.

Chapter one

In this chapter we explore the current state of the People Professional market and outline some of the challenges that lie ahead. We look at the views being expressed through research, via leading figures in the People Professional market and by looking at what the professional institutes who represent us have to say about the future. We discover that the overall picture isn't that rosy and we begin to learn about the role that alignment has to play in achieving long-term success.

Chapter two

Before you can achieve successful alignment you need to ensure that you have the right skills to succeed. In this chapter we look at what those skills are and explain the role they have to play in setting you up to achieve alignment. We discover that 'good enough' can reap massive rewards and explore the psyche of senior managers to discover that, despite what you may think or want, they care very little about how you do something, as long as you get the results.

Chapter three

Knowing the market you operate within is essential if you want to be successful. In this chapter we explore some of the facts behind the market we operate in and challenge the ways in which we measure the size of these markets.

Chapter four

Sustainability has become something of a buzz-word of late and for many it's seen as little more than "tree hugging". But sustainability in the true sense of the word is all about making sure that your business stays in business for year after year after year. In this chapter we explore the steps you'll need to take to ensure that your business can achieve success on an on going basis and avoid becoming the next Woolworth, Ferranti, TWA or Allied Carpets.

Chapter five

Great meals are the result of great recipes. It's the same with business. In this chapter we explore the recipe for business success and look at the fundamental building blocks that make for an aligned and successful business.

Chapter six

Strategy is the first of the fundamental alignment building blocks. In this chapter we look at why understanding the strategy of your business is important and why developing an aligned strategy is absolutely critical. We look at how to develop a great strategy and constantly remind ourselves about the overriding importance of putting the needs of your business, rather than yourself, at the heart of your strategy.

Chapter seven

Structure is the second of the fundamental alignment building blocks. In this chapter we'll look at making sure that you're set up to operate in a lean and fast manner by ensuring that your structure does not get in the way of you doing business. We'll challenge the stupidity of approaching problems with traditional "management speak" and show how by making your structure fit for business you'll stand the best chance of achieving alignment.

Chapter eight

Culture is the third of the fundamental alignment building blocks. In this chapter we'll look at the importance and impact of the right culture on your business and on your ability to achieve alignment. We'll explore business values and even challenge major businesses to see if they live by the values they supposedly hold dear to their hearts. We'll also explore setting appropriate goals and ensuring that you create a sense of ownership and responsibility within your business.

Chapter nine

Execution is the last of the fundamental alignment building blocks. In this chapter we look at why talk is cheap and execution is everything. We'll explore the ways in which you can increase your ability to execute (deliver) and how you can reduce meaningless effort in your business to ensure that your people are as productive as possible.

Chapter ten

In this chapter we explore the remaining aspects that go together to make great alignment. We'll explore some of the myths behind finding the right talent, we'll look at the importance of leadership, we'll explore the impact of innovation and we'll consider the effect of mergers and partnerships on your business.

Chapter eleven

Measuring success within the People profession is never easy. In this chapter we'll explore the ways in which the People Profession is measured and we'll discover the common mistakes that are often made. We'll explore the building blocks of measurement including data, metrics, deltas, indicators, KPIs and much more. We'll also draw out the differences between the different types of metrics.

Chapter twelve

In the final chapter we'll be drawing together the learning from all the previous chapters and looking at practical examples of how you can measure alignment within your business and how you can identify areas for improvement. There's even an example questionnaire for you so you can get started right away.

Chapter activities

At the end of each chapter you'll find a series of activities which helps embed the learning and begins to draw together all the key elements for you to achieve alignment within your business.

Appendices

There are four appendices which provide further reading and information and support some of the business stories told in this book.

References

And finally there is a section where all of the books and publications referred to in this book are listed.

Acknowledgements

Getting a book from that germ of an idea to something you can hold in your hand is, I have found, far easier said than done. In getting to that point where I can actually say "It's done" the following people should be thanked:

To Liggy Webb for initiating my thoughts when she said "You know what, you should write a book."

To Camilla Straghan, Sarah Roberts, Clare Cassar and the rest of the Cheltenham 'team' for putting up with books and papers strewn over the kitchen night after night.

To Alison Neale, The Proof Fairy for turning around a manuscript with such speed and accuracy.

To David Pardo of Pardo Fox for his knowledge and insights into the UK People Professional market.

To Colin Gautrey for his time and experience for setting me up for success with my first book, and to Perry Timms for seeing the real value of my words and reassuring me that this book really will have a practical and lasting impact for all People Professionals.

And last but by no means least, immense thanks to Anne Field for her continuous encouragement, wit and perseverance at tackling my rather shaky, if not unique punctuation.

Jonathan Kettleborough

November 2012

1

The State We're In

"It is not the strongest of the species that survives, nor the most intelligent that survives. It is the one that is the most adaptable to change."

Charles Darwin
British scientist who laid the foundations of the theory of evolution and transformed the way we think about the natural world.

We're hanging on by our fingertips!

Sometimes there's just no point writing a fancy introduction or pulling punches and this is one of those times.

I've been actively involved with the Training, Talent, HR, Learning and Development industry (the People Profession) for almost thirty years and during that time I've seen virtually every new trend in the book, every fabulous promise, every version of the "silver bullet" and quite a few versions of the "emperor's new clothes." But I have yet to see the People Function truly deliver on their promises or their potential.

I honestly feel that elements of the People Function within a true business context are close to disappearing, maybe forever. I believe that unless we radically and rapidly change our approaches then the People Function could forever lose its ability to add value within businesses and I honestly believe we're close to that point now.

I'm not trying to plot the demise of an industry I love and that has supported me for many years. I love this industry because of the stunning results it can achieve; I just know that we've lost our way. We've become too focused on theory and fads and I feel we're in real danger of disappearing up our own social-media-blended-learning-synchronous-business-partner backsides.

We are **not** in a good place.

We have two options

As People Professionals we have two simple but fundamental options:

1. we can carry on the way we are and face our potential demise, or
2. we can make the choice to survive and prosper by changing where necessary to align with our businesses and customers and serve them in the manner they deserve.

The choice is entirely ours. One route will almost certainly lead to our demise; the other has the potential to lead us into a much better long-term position.

As John Harvey Jones once said, "Standing still is not an option," and this is certainly no time for us to stand still.

We must make a difference to the businesses we serve; for if we don't then what's the point of us doing anything?

We must align, we must serve,
we must deliver!

The Goal, the Holy Grail, the Promised Land

As People Professionals (the term I'll be using throughout this book to describe the Training, Talent, HR, Learning and Development industries), we want to add real value to our businesses and customers, we want to get the investment we deserve for our projects, we want to be approached by senior executives to solve complex business problems and we want to be thanked and praised by our Managing Director / Chief Executive Officer for all the positive changes we make.

We want to be heard.

We want to be respected.

We want a seat at the table.

But for most of us this just isn't happening.

And have you ever wondered why?

I mean **really** wondered why?

Have you ever wondered **why** you're not in the position you want to be, why you're fighting for face-time with executives and customers, why people look at you with strange expressions when you explain what you do and why your budgets are almost always the first to be cut?

Be honest, you have; we all have. And unless we make the dramatic changes outlined in this book we will always be fighting for face-time, for realistic budgets and for an opportunity to make the difference we know we can.

It's time to make the change!

The reality of where we're at

In this chapter I'll set out the dire position our industry is currently in and explain the reality of our own situation. Before some of you shout out, I know that there are pockets of real excellence out there; there always will be, but they are just that, pockets. There's good practice out there and there are some really great results being delivered but we are failing to act as an industry and we are failing on a massive scale to capitalise on our potential for the following reasons:

- for starters, our own industry doesn't think we're doing a good job
- industry observers don't think we're doing a good job
- big businesses don't think we're doing a good job
- we don't even do the things **we** say are important
- and to cap it all, we say that alignment is the number one priority and **still** fail to do anything about it.

We can make the change and realise the true potential of our industry but it's going to be an interesting journey.

Where's the support from our own industry?

It's one thing for outsiders to moan about our achievements, but after all what do they know about what we do? How could they ever understand the complexity of what we have to deliver, of the pressure we work under and the challenges we face? On the other hand, when our **own** industry starts moaning and criticising what we do then we're in real trouble. And you know what, **we're in real trouble!**

In the April 2012 issue of People Management, the magazine of the Chartered Institute of Personnel and Development (CIPD), Bill Parsons, CIPD vice-president wrote:

> "I have often heard fellow HR professionals questioning why their firms don't take Learning and Development (L&D) more seriously or appreciate the strategic benefits of investing in it. I'm sure there are many reasons for this, but too often it's because we focus on the Return on Investment (ROI) for a specific tactical initiative or an individual's development needs, rather than making the connection to company-wide capability and the wider, long-term business strategy and future success of the organisation."

Bill concluded his article by saying,

"Demonstrating direct connection between L&D and financial success is always going to be difficult. Conceptual models can seem somewhat flaky. But without some kind of model we will never train ourselves to consider economic as much as, or more than, the physiological or sociological benefits. If we want to be taken seriously, we must think and talk strategy and even economics at every level."

Considering that Bill represents the world's largest HR community with over 135,000 members in 120 countries this is pretty damning stuff!

But perhaps Don Taylor, Chairman of the Learning and Performance Institute which represents 10,000 members and over 1,000 accredited companies thinks differently?

Well, eh, no!

In part of his 2010 article for the Charity Learning Consortium Don said:

"The opportunity is clear: at last training should be able to take the initiative and prove its value to the organisation. It should be able to embed learning in the fabric of daily life.

The threat is simple: if we don't do this, others will. Others less able, with less understanding of learning, people who believe that anyone can facilitate learning, because after all, we all went to school, didn't we? That's like saying that anyone can be Shakespeare because we can all write."

Don concluded his article by saying,

"L&D has to aim higher than ever before. Of course we will always act professionally, but now we have to demonstrate it. We have to show that we have the right frameworks for creating a learning organisation, for demonstrating value, for adding to the business.

Quite simply, we have to drive ourselves on to be the best in our field. That way, we will be the agent of personal and organizational development that we really can be. Without this drive to professionalism, we run the risk of irrelevance.

It's up to us."

This is incredible. Two people representing over 145,000 "People Professionals" who between them are clearly saying that we don't get it, we don't get business, we don't get strategy, we don't demonstrate value and as a result we're not being taken seriously.

Not a great start for our profession, is it?

Where's the support from industry observers?

So our own industry isn't that supportive of our efforts and nor are industry observers. Keith Hammonds famously wrote in his "Fast Company" article entitled "Why we hate HR":

> "Let's face it: After close to 20 years of hopeful rhetoric about becoming "strategic partners" with a "seat at the table" where the business decisions that matter are made, most human resources professionals aren't nearly there. They have no seat, and the table is locked inside a conference room to which they have no key. HR people are, for most practical purposes, neither strategic nor leaders."

Although the excerpt I've taken from Keith's article is talking about "HR people," if you read the full article you'll realise he's talking about all forms of People Professionals. So yet again this is pretty damning stuff; it's certainly not a great place to be and it's a pretty poor reflection on the industry.

This is crazy . . . . there just **has** to be some good news . . . somewhere!

I searched for good news, but much of it was rather broad "motherhood and apple pie" statements which could apply to just about anything. Instead I continued to find more and more disparaging statements about the industry. In his paper, "Maximize Training Impact by Aligning Learning with Business Goals" Jay Bahlis goes for the jugular by stating that:

- less than 10% of training expenditures actually result in transfer to the job.
- most of the knowledge and skills eventually gained through training (well over 80% by some estimates) is not fully applied on-the-job. By some accounts, less than 30% of what is learned (in training) actually gets used on the job.
- in an effort to reduce costs and focus on core business, organisations such as Nortel Networks, Goodyear, and others, are outsourcing training management, training development, training delivery, and training administration and support.

So, more damning evidence supporting the fact that as a People Profession we haven't yet got our act together. I mean, after all, how could anyone even begin to think we're doing a good job if we can't look after appropriate budgets, can't deliver effective interventions? As a result we're in danger of being outsourced. Sound familiar?

But surely the big businesses, the ones with the big People Departments and the budgets and the fancy training and development programmes must think differently. As major investors in people they **must** appreciate the effect that great and effective people can have? You'd have thought so, but no!

Where's the support from big businesses?

Big businesses spend millions of pounds on their People Function every year, both in terms of direct spend and the internal costs of releasing people to be developed and coached. Businesses make this investment (you would have thought) in the hope that they reap some reward for their time, effort and trouble. But can you imagine if, after making such a massive commitment, these businesses felt their efforts were failing to deliver results? That would be one hell of a shock—wouldn't it?

But in 2010 just such a situation occurred. In a report by Capita, 100 out of the top 500 UK companies were asked about their L&D departments. Only 18% of the businesses surveyed felt they had People Departments (specifically Learning and Development) that were operationally aligned to the business.

Ouch!

It makes me wonder what on earth the other 82% are doing; what they are spending their businesses' hard-earned money on and why, when it's clear that their role is to serve the business, they don't!

The painfully revealing details from the report said that:

- the majority (70%) of business leaders fear that inadequate staff skills are the greatest threat to their ability to capitalise on the recovery.

  At the time of writing this book (during mid-2012) the UK had been officially declared as entering a double-dip recession and with clearly a mountain to climb for so many businesses, how dare the People Function fail their businesses at such a critical time!

- more than two thirds of business leaders admit that their under-trained workforce is struggling to cope with expanded job remits following waves of job cutting during the recession.

  So why aren't People Professionals fixing this problem?

- over a third of leaders (36%) lack confidence that their employees have the skills required to deliver the firm's upturn strategy, with close to half (46%) casting doubt on their L&D department's ability to provide these learning services.

So if the HR department can't supply the right people and the L&D department can't provide the learning services, who on earth can? And if these departments **can't** deliver, is it any wonder that so many of them are in danger of being outsourced?

- over half (55%) claim that their firm is failing to deliver the necessary training for recovery.

What??!! This is what People Professionals **do**, so why aren't they doing it? And if they aren't doing it then just what **are** they doing? Perhaps, like Nero, they are fiddling while Rome burns.

- more than half (52%) describe their L&D function as slow to respond to the changing requirements of their business during economic turbulence.

Clearly, People Functions that are slow to respond are just not aligned with, or in touch with their business, and this is totally unacceptable.

- as strategic objectives have evolved, close to half (46%) of senior managers report no significant change in the training delivery to their workforce. Going forward, almost as many (43%) expect no significant change to L&D delivery over the next two to three years.

So what are the People Functions doing? Are they sitting on their hands, filing their nails, attending meaningless conferences (more of this later)? Don't L&D understand the business and respond to it in a timely fashion?

- the vast majority (82%) of leaders lack confidence that their firm's L&D strategy and delivery are aligned to the company's operational strategy. Half (50%) believe that their L&D function is stuck in a 'business as usual' mindset.

And here's the rub: L&D (yet again) are failing to understand the needs of the business.

And the concluding remarks of the Capita report said,

> "The clear message is that L&D is failing to adapt to the changing needs of UK plc."

In pure pound note terms Capita estimates that this equates to a 21% shortfall in productivity estimated at an annual cost of £35.7 billion to the UK's largest firms!

Ouch . . . again!

So it's more and more and more bad news for the People Profession. The institutes that represent our profession feel we're doing a bad job, key industry observers feel we're doing a bad job and major companies feel we're doing a bad job. Perhaps we really are doomed to extinction?

And just when I thought it couldn't get any worse—when I thought we'd reached the deep, dark bottom of the barrel—I have to tell you the disturbing, utterly crazy, stupid, unbelievable and totally insane fact that the People Industry doesn't act upon what it clearly knows is the right direction in which to go! How mad is that?

We don't even believe the writing on our own wall!

For many People Professionals, words like "business" and "performance" and "profit" are dirty words and tough ones at that! People Professionals would seemingly prefer to spend their time messing about with the minutiae of the subject, the deep psychology of learning, the new models and theories of instructional design, the "new" way to measure IQ/EQ and the "new" application of QR codes.

Don't believe me? . . . . Then read on . . .

According to the 2009 survey by the Learning and Skills Group (LSG), an online community of over 5,000 People Professionals, over 86% of respondents thought that there needed to be "A stronger link between learning and development and core business processes and strategy."

In the same survey, when asked "What is your personal single greatest learning challenge at present?" the highest response by over one in four people was "Aligning learning to organisational objectives".

Given this depth of feeling and understanding you'd have thought the LSG forums would be buzzing with people discussing business strategy and alignment, wouldn't you?

Unfortunately (as you've probably already guessed) this is not the case. Search through many of the People-related forums (across a wide range of applicable sites) and you'll find precious little talk about business, but more than enough talk about:

- content strategies
- mobile learning
- content and digital media curation
- social media—LOTS on this one!
- iPads and how they will change
- the face of learning the best software for HR, podcasting, screen capture, training records etc.
- typing pools—yes, I kid you not!
- mothers and careers

And, as I'm sure you can imagine, the list goes on, and on, and on . . .

So I have to ask all People Professionals, what on earth are you doing? Why do you feel so able to articulate the **most** important issues, and then seem totally unwilling to do something about them? And given that you **say** you know what's important I'd have thought that the various conferences aimed at People Professionals would have reflected that, wouldn't you?

No!

In April 2012, the CIPD held its annual Learning and Development exhibition; over 70 conference sessions dedicated to L&D. There were seminars dedicated to the use of technology (naturally enough) and social media (here we go again) and Tweetups and mentoring and so on.

But guess how many seminars dealt with the impact of L&D on the business, or L&D alignment, or L&D strategy . . . ?

None!

And it doesn't end there—well, did you honestly think it would? The highly popular Learning Technologies Conference held in London in January of each year hosts around forty top flight seminars and speakers. And the number of sessions dedicated to business impact (as can best be gleaned from the 2012 conference programme)?

About two!

As I'm finishing this book, details of the 2013 Learning Technologies Conference have just been announced. According to the publicity the conference features "Over 50 of the learning industry's foremost speakers, thinkers, visionaries and practitioners". And as before, how many sessions are dedicated to business impact (as can best be gleaned from the conference programme)?

About two!

The TrainingZone Live 2012 Conference held in May attracted delegates to an agenda of twenty one sessions and workshops. How many sessions were dedicated to business or strategy or alignment or anything but the "how-do-we-make-ourselves-better-and-do-better-things-with-content-or-technology-or-anything-but-business"?

None!

And I even checked the Twitter feed from the day and analysed the hashtag (#tzl12). The five most popular words . . .

Need, Learning, Delivery, Technology and Training

Do you think that business, strategy or alignment got a look in at all? Of course not!

The recently established Learning and Performance Institute (LPI) has over ten thousand members and over one thousand accredited companies. Grown out of the Institute for IT Training (IITT) the LPI is positioning itself at the forefront of People Development within the UK. As I write this book, the LPI's annual Learning Live conference line-up has just been announced; two days of digital this and mobile that but yet again precious little in terms of pure business issues or alignment.

Deep down, beneath the veneer of content strategies and PowerPoint slides with automated Tweets we all know that we need to align our People Function to our businesses and to our customers. We know that when we talk to non People Professional folks they look at us as though we're speaking a foreign language (we often are) and we know that unless we change our gameplay we will be doomed to extinction. Don't take my word for it; here's David Wood, Editor of HR Magazine:

> "HR (People) professionals must evolve into being the best thinkers about the human and organisational side of the business. Business is dramatically changing. Changes are occurring in virtually every element of the social, political, and economic environments that affect business. They include technology, globalisation, communications, regulations, competitiveness, demographics, shareholder demands and a tight market for key talent."

Hear, hear David!

The truth is out there . . . if only we'd take a better look

In February 2012, the Chartered Management Institute (CMI) in conjunction with Penna published "The Business Benefits of Management and Leadership Development (MLD)". In the same month, HR Magazine said of the CMI/Penna report:

> "The findings also show high performing organisations spend on average 36% more on management and leadership development per manager per year than low performing ones (£1,738 compared to £1,275)."

Christopher Kinsella, acting chief executive for CMI, said:

> "The good news is that organisations who are investing strategically in management and leadership development are far more likely to be reaping the benefits through higher performance . . . . by investing in management and leadership development wisely, employers can make a real, measurable difference."

And what do you think has been the take-away that many of the People Profession's "great and good" have adopted from this report?

They've reiterated how "better" businesses invest more in MLD (as promoted in the report), but then have gone on to suggest that by investing more money you'll somehow automatically make your business better!

Really?

It may look like the same thing, but it isn't!

If we follow this train of thought then we'd find that "better performing" businesses also spend more money on salaries and office accommodation and flights and travel and pensions and biscuits and highlighter pens and even Post-It notes!

. . . and therefore by investing more in pensions, biscuits and Post-It notes we would naturally build more successful companies! What utter rubbish!

It's not about how much you invest . . . It's about how you manage the investment!

And the "great and good" within the People Profession have **totally** missed the key point of this report. And I mean **TOTALLY**.

Much of the publicity surrounding the report has focused on the issue of companies only being successful because they invest in MLD yet the real and lasting message from this report first appeared in the foreword on page three, which said:

> "Top performing companies align their development practices
> closely to their business strategy and they evaluate the effects of
> their investment more thoroughly."

Oooh, there it is . . .

That "hidden" word which People Professionals seem so keen to ignore . . .

Align

At last, a little light starts to shine.

Let's return to some of the final words from the Capita report, which state that:

> "UK plc urgently needs to adopt a strategic approach to people
> development, one highly aligned with overall business goals."

Oooh, there it is again . . .

That magic word . . .

Aligned

My word, People Professionals aligned with the business; surely not? Surely that's just fun and frolics and conjecture and stupidity?

Or maybe not . . . .

According to the 2007 report by the Aberdeen Group called "Learning & Development Aligning Workforce with Business", those businesses that achieve workforce alignment enjoy a 77% increase in employee productivity. The same report showed that:

- 43% of all businesses cite the need to align their workforce with business objectives as the number one pressure driving learning and development.
- the Best-in-Class are nearly twice as likely as their peers to have a learning and development strategy that is integrated with the business' overall strategic plan.
- the Best-in-Class are 68% more likely than laggards and 39% more likely than the industry average to get HR and training personnel into the business units in order to understand business needs and priorities.

And yet again, that oh-so-special word . . .

Alignment

I'm starting to find this strangely compelling; as soon as I see the "align" word associated with People Professionals then the results get better, stronger and deeper. Perhaps this whole alignment agenda has something to offer us after all . . .

Bersin & Associates, in their high-impact Learning Culture 2010 reports, show that businesses with a stronger learning culture and alignment of the People Function to the business delivered better business results, not just in one or two "natural People areas" but in areas such as:

- innovation
- employee productivity
- customer satisfaction
- market share.

So here we are again, more and more clear evidence (as though it were actually needed) that aligning the People Function to business needs and strategies gains results.

A is for Alignment

Alignment. Not a big word, and to be brutally honest not a word that you'll see mentioned that much in the People world, but as we've seen, oh what an important word it is!

One definition of alignment is:

> "The process of adjusting parts so that they are in proper relative position."

I love this definition; it's simple and says it all—putting the right parts in the right places.

Align

Aligning

Alignment

According to the CMI/Penna report:

"High performing organisations have significantly higher levels
of alignment . . . This suggests that the alignment between HR
and business strategy is a key differentiator between higher and
lower performing organisations."

See that? Not spending more but aligning what you have.

WOW! So this alignment "thing" could really make a difference for People
Professionals; a major difference. But, for a moment, let's step outside
the often insular world of the People Professional to see what the wider
business community thinks about alignment:

- according to Fred Smith, Chairman of FedEx, "Most managers
  don't know what alignment is all about; alignment is the essence
  of management."
- KPMG research as long ago as 2001 identified that "Getting
  everyone aligned around strategies and vision was endorsed by
  87% of US and European senior executives as their top priority."

Alignment. It's like all of a sudden realising that you might actually hit the
target if you bothered to point the gun in the right direction!

And that's what the remainder of this book is all about: identifying exactly
how you can align yourself, your department or your company to the
needs of the market. By achieving this alignment I believe you will begin
to reap the rewards that you and your business have desired for so long.

Wanting to be heard. Wanting to be respected. Wanting a seat
at the table.

Seeing eye-to-eye

Despite what many books and publications may lead you to think,
alignment is not a one-way street. It's not just about making sure that you
have all your ducks in a row; it's also about making sure that your business

and customers recognise this fact and recognise that you have real value to offer; it's about seeing eye-to-eye.

When you're seeing eye-to-eye with your business and customers you understand and respond to their needs in an appropriate and timely manner. Your solutions make sense; your request for resources are understood and met and your business and customers recognise the value you're delivering.

Alignment is unselfish; it's not about you, or your department, or your hobby-horse projects, or the latest fads and fashions; it's about driving success within your business and your customers. When you're aligned you're not fighting for face-time or resources or fighting outsourcing deals, you're a valued and integral part of your business; you have a seat at the table and you're heard and respected.

Conclusions

Wonderful news; all this is possible. Yes, there's effort needed. Yes, it'll be tough. Yes, there are some real hurdles and barriers to overcome. However, the future is in your hands and should you choose to approach this issue head on, then it's clear that you can deliver some real results. It doesn't matter if you're an individual, or if you're running an internal People Function or even a commercial People business; alignment can and does offer you the real chance of making a deep and lasting change.

Join with me as I take you on the journey towards this amazing transformation.

Chapter 1: Activities

As you've seen in this chapter, not everyone thinks the People Profession is as good as it could be, but what does your business or customers think?

Take some time to talk to people you really trust; perhaps they are customers, or perhaps they are colleagues within your business. Ask them what they think of People Professionals and the People Function.

Write down the key words and phrases they use, both good and bad, and make a note of them here:

Positive Phrases	Negative Phrases

Ask them what they would like People Professionals to do differently and make a note of these here:

The things People Professionals could do differently

We'll come back to the things you've noted later on.

2

Setting Yourself Up For Success

"When written in Chinese, the word "crisis" is composed of two characters. One represents danger and the other represents opportunity."

John F. Kennedy
35th President of the United States

Introduction

Throughout my career I've had the pleasure of working with some truly wonderful and influential people. I've worked with CEOs, operations directors, sales directors, top scientists and engineers and hard-nosed entrepreneurs. The thing I've noticed about all of them, no matter what age, male or female, young or old, is the way they . . .

Keep everything simple

It doesn't matter what the subject is, they just manage to keep it simple. Here's a great example. I once consulted for a major UK nuclear company—I'll leave you to work out which one. I was having a conversation with two of their top scientists, both PhDs and with years and years of experience in what they do. One was trying to explain to me the conditions inside a nuclear reactor. He was using a number of scientific terms which I clearly didn't understand. His boss (who was standing watching) looked at me and said, "Jonathan, it's like this. Imagine carbon dioxide under such pressure that it's the consistency of pea soup." I nodded, amazed that I actually understood what he was describing. "Well," he continued, "we take that pea soup and throw it round the inside of the reactor at the speed of a tornado."

I didn't need to be a scientist to realise this was a pretty hostile environment and of course (as I'm recounting this story to you) it's stayed with me for many years because in my experience the average People Professional often has difficulty in simplifying the complex.

But simplicity is something we must seek; that and the truth. No longer are our employers and clients willing to listen to us bleating on about the latest fads and gizmos and what we **think** is the best thing to do because it feels good to us. No, we have to begin talking to people in terms **they** understand and delivering real results for **them**—over and over again.

If you want to know where alignment really begins then take a look in the mirror because it begins with **you**! You are the starting point and unless you begin to set yourself up for success then you will not only find this journey exceptionally hard, but you are also likely to fail. As People Professionals you all know the value that a good leader brings to a business; this is the chance for you to develop your 'alignment leadership skills'.

In this chapter I'll be talking about how you can set yourself up for success with your business or customers. It's important that you thoroughly understand these issues before we get into the detail of aligning with your business otherwise there's a danger of over-complicating what is actually a very simple process.

In this chapter I'll cover the need for you to:

- deliver something rather than nothing
- talk the language of business
- solve REAL business problems
- be a practical polymath
- invest in your skills
- understand technology like a kid
- fail fast

So let's get started by looking at some of the underpinning skills you'll need to make alignment a real success.

Deliver something rather than nothing

I'm sure that many of you have seen the famous sketch from the Monty Python film "The Life of Brian"—the one where John Cleese looks at the assembled plotters and, while lambasting the Romans, says:

> "They've taken everything we had, not just from us, from our fathers and from our fathers' fathers . . . . And what have they ever given us in return?"

I'll not repeat the whole sketch word for word but the plotters begin to list the things the Romans have given them. Things like:

- the aqueduct
- sanitation
- roads
- medicine
- education
- health
- irrigation
- wine
- public baths, and
- public safety.

And the sketch ends with that magic statement from Mr Cleese:

> "All right . . . all right . . . but apart from better sanitation and medicine and education and irrigation and public health and roads and a freshwater system and baths and public order . . . what have the Romans ever done for us?"

OK, I'll be the first to admit that Monty Python isn't normally quoted in books about People Professionals, but let's stop for a moment and think . . . If your senior managers or clients were to look you in the eye and ask "So what have you ever done for us?" could you answer them with a list of fine achievements?

So skill number one that you need to understand is that in order to be successful you need to deliver **something** of value to your business or customers. Promises of 'better' just don't generate revenue and profit.

Here's a situation for you to think about. Suppose that you were on a boat, far out at sea, and for some reason you fell overboard. Would you like to wait for someone to design and develop the ideal personal sea survival vehicle, complete with food, warm clothes and satellite tracking systems, or would you, right now, prefer someone to throw you a decent sized piece of wood to cling on to?

My guess is that you'd prefer the piece of wood rather than waiting. It isn't ideal but it does a bloody good job—for now. And so it is with business.

Perhaps what you deliver may not be as wonderful and polished as it could be, but it'll be good enough. And in business 'good enough' has built fortunes. Consider Microsoft, for example. It wasn't until version 3 that Windows began to deliver something decent, albeit those within the Mac community **still** don't think Windows matches what they have. And although Microsoft has suffered a 6% decline in revenues at its Windows division as competition from smartphones and tablet computers increases, combined with dented worldwide sales of personal computers, they **still** made £3bn in the three months ending 31 December 2011. And as Microsoft makes £4 of operating profit from every £6 of revenue from Windows then this 'good enough' product is certainly delivering healthy returns.

So you see, delivering something is always better than delivering nothing. And the message to take away from this section is:

Delivering 'good enough' can reap massive rewards.

Talk the language of business

This is a bold statement but in my experience People Professionals generally don't always 'get' business or speak its language and seem rather unwilling to educate themselves in this area, preferring instead to stick to babble about "context-driven learning strategies," or "ten reasons to use Moodle" or whatever else seems to be the hot topic of the day.

I once worked with a hard-nosed entrepreneur. Each day he would ask me the same question: "What are you doing to make me money today?" Now **that's** the language of business!

As People Professionals you need to understand this language. Not from a point of walking around spouting how you're aiming to "deliver a step change in EBITDA" but from a position where people in the business really get what value you're adding. I'll be taking you through the development of value propositions later in the book but for now you need to do everything you can to drop the "pink and fluffy people speak" and talk business instead.

Keith Hammonds (who I mentioned earlier) wrote about one experience where he was listening to a presentation entitled "From Technicians to Consultants: How to Transform Your HR Staff into Strategic Business Partners". Keith said of his experience:

> "I have no idea what she's talking about. There is mention of 'internal action learning' and 'being more planful in my approach.' I hear about 'initiatives in performance management, organisation design, and horizontal-solutions teams . . . leveraging internal resources and involving external resources'."

Be brutally honest with yourself. Do you use statements similar to those above? The chances are that you do, so bloody well cut them out!

Let's try something for a moment. Let's suppose that you were going to a conference full of like-minded People folks. Take a piece of paper and write down the top five things you would talk to them about if you had a few minutes of their undivided attention.

Done that? OK, now read on . . .

A PR Week survey focusing on CEO communication found that over 24% of CEOs said that they should spend between 21% and 30% of their time communicating with employees face-to-face. In the same survey, 55% of CEOs said they spend more time communicating than they did two years ago. And with this focus on communication, especially face-to-face, you can be sure that at some point you'll have the opportunity of making your mark; just be sure you're well prepared!

Let's return to the list you made a few moments ago. Although not a perfect science, it's quite likely that you've listed one or more of the following:

- Size of budget and projects
- Attracting and recruiting the best candidates
- Training facilities
- Number of staff in your department
- Issues with employment law
- Social media
- Blended learning
- E-learning
- Talent management
- Return on Investment
- Awards and prizes.

And if you did write down a few of the above it's hardly surprising. After all, you're talking to your peers who will naturally already speak a similar language to you.

Now think about how your CEO communicates. If he or she was meeting the CEO of another company for lunch and really wanted to impress them, what might be the key messages they'd be sure to try and get across? As before, make a short list of these.

Again, although not a perfect science, it's highly likely that you've listed one or more of the following:

- Market opportunities and threats
- Revenues and profit
- Alignment
- Creating added value
- Share price
- Strategy

But let's just stop for a moment and consider the underlying communication issue. If you were presenting information to your CEO, what would you focus on? The truth is, you'd almost certainly stick to what you know (the operational and delivery issues) and deliver it with a smile and your fingers crossed! But what does the CEO want to hear? Clearly, as they're focused on revenues, profits, value-added etc., they'll want to know how the People Function is assisting them in meeting their goals. This is one of the most critical issues of all; in order to communicate effectively it's essential that you use the same focus, words and terminology as your CEO. Anything less and your message will not have the impact it deserves; and of course you can only deliver great messages if you **really** understand your business.

Solve REAL business problems

Here's a shocking statement for you . . .

Senior managers don't really give a damn about social media or facilitation techniques or learning design. They just want solutions to their business problems—and fast.

The book "Tough Choices or Tough Times: The Report of the New Commission on the Skills of the American Workforce" says that:

"The days of achieving ever increasing efficiencies are drawing to a close. We now need to equip organisations for innovation rather than just reaching for the next optimisation, and this means solving real problems—fast."

Just think about this for a moment . . .

Solving real problems . . . Fast.

When was the last time you heard an operations director asking for a social media based intervention with real-time Tweets from a web-based PowerPoint presentation? Probably never. Senior managers and customers state their problems and then say they want them fixed. They don't really care how (within reason of course), they just want them fixed. And this, as People Professionals, is what you should be responding to, always.

I recall sitting in business school for my first ever lecture which was on the subject of production and operations management. In walked the professor who smiled and said:

"You're faced with a hundred things that aren't working in your business; which ones do you fix first?"

A massive light bulb went on for me. Of course you can't fix everything; you must pick the issues that'll have the greatest impact and work on those. Focus on these issues and nothing else.

People Professionals need to understand this. They need to solve **real** problems that customers and businesses have, not the ones that the People Professionals want to work on. People Professionals have an overwhelming plethora of the most wonderfully named tools and techniques but we have to remember to focus on the problem in hand and not on trying to deploy tools or techniques just because we have them.

Be a practical polymath

I talked earlier about a situation where I'd asked you to imagine that you'd fallen overboard from a boat far out at sea. The solution, for the time being, was to hang on to a large piece of wood.

I'm returning to this example because the piece of wood was an immediately practical and cost-effective solution. Sure, it wasn't going to last forever but it worked and it **was** practical.

By its nature, being a People Professional is all about solving everyday problems and creating practical solutions. As you'll see as you work through this book, aligning with your business and customers is about understanding and solving problems. But problems can be solved in one of two ways: they can be solved in simple, practical ways or in complex and over-engineered ways. Which one do you think your customers or business would prefer?

I mentioned that you needed to be a practical polymath without explaining what one was. Polymath is Greek for "having learned much" and a polymath is therefore a person whose expertise spans a significant number of different subject areas. That doesn't necessarily mean they hold a bagful of fancy qualifications, but they know a whole bunch of things on a whole range of subjects; the sort of person you'd readily select for your pub quiz team!

In order to be a practical problem solver you'll need to have a wide body of knowledge. As a People Professional you should naturally know about recruitment, selection, employment law, adult learning theories, technology, learning design and all the detailed aspects of your chosen specialism, but you should also understand maths, strategy, finance, logistics, global markets, skills, talent and so on. No longer can the People Professional be confined to the classroom, workshop, computer screen or meeting room. You need to move from being tools-based to being solutions-based and you can't offer practical solutions without a very broad range of knowledge.

Invest in YOUR skills

I'll bet you've heard the term "cobbler's children"? Like the proverbial children of the shoemaker who go without shoes because the cobbler is too busy fixing the shoes of other people, within businesses I'm sure you've come across many instances where technology companies have outdated systems, where marketing companies either don't market themselves or don't understand the latest social media tools or where consulting firms fail to put into practice for themselves a single theory or model upon which they have built their reputation.

Sounds familiar?

Well what about you? Yes, **you**? What are **you** doing to add to **your** skills?

Something?

Anything?

Nothing?

According to research by McKinsey, the Centre for Economic Performance and the London School of Economics—and hold on tight here—better educated managers run better businesses! Let me say that again in case you missed it the first time . . .

Better educated managers run better businesses

I realise that this is probably a massive case of "stating the bleedin' obvious" because as People Professionals you will (of course) understand the value of education and skills in contributing to the success of a business. But back to my earlier question—what about **you**? When did **you** last invest in **yourself** and add to **your** portfolio of skills?

The chances are it'll be a while ago, if at all. And I'm not talking about attending the odd conference or two and sitting at the back of the room or participating in a webinar; I'm talking about gathering real, hard and tangible skills—ideally in something related to understanding business.

We have a big hill to climb. According to the McKinsey research I mentioned earlier, the average percentage of UK managers with a degree is just 43.3%—that puts the UK at the bottom of the pile. Greece, Portugal and Italy are above us, as are Sweden, France, the US, Germany, Poland and Japan. Now I know that just because you have a degree doesn't necessarily make you a great manager, but it's a strong indication of the talent available. Compare our 43.3% of managers with a degree to 70% in Japan—it almost doesn't bear thinking about.

According to a survey by Hays (February 2011), 61% of workers complained that their employer is not doing enough to invest in their skills. But this is not a one-way street and employees should ignore the issue at their peril.

The Hays survey revealed that over half (55%) of workers in the private sector do not know, or are unsure about, the skills employers are likely to demand in the next five years. Over half (58%) report that the skills required for their current roles are already changing and just under half (46%) are concerned that their current skill set will be insufficient to meet employers' expectations in five years' time.

Clearly there's a need for People Professionals to ensure they gain and retain the skills they need both now and for the future in order to ensure they are best placed to contribute to their business.

Understand technology like a kid

You just can't escape technology these days. The amount of technology that's come along in recent years is just mind-blowing. As best we can establish, as a human race we've been on this planet for around 200,000 years. If we represented that time as just 24 hours, then email, Facebook, the internet, Twitter, Pinterest, iPhones and iPads have arrived within the last five seconds. That's quite a rate of change!

The way you handle, deal with and talk about technology within a business will be crucial to the People Function becoming accepted and delivering real performance improvements. As with so many other things, the senior managers don't give a damn what technology you're using; it's the results that count. So this means focusing on outputs rather than boring the pants off people by telling them how clever you are that you've integrated your Learning Management System with Twitter via an iPad App which also links to and automatically updates your employee self-service HR system. Frankly, who cares!

Look at how kids handle technology—they just pick it up and use it, they don't really care how it works, and they'll only use it as long as it delivers benefits for them; it's about making use of technology rather than just using it for the sake of it. Tell a senior manager that you've saved money or solved their problem and that's all that matters. And it's all that will ever matter.

Fail fast

There's an old saying that 'Success breeds success'. However, according to Professor Vinit Desai from the University of Colorado Denver Business School, success may be sweeter, but failure is the greater teacher. Vinit said,

> "We found that the knowledge gained from success was often fleeting while knowledge from failure stuck around for years."

I'm not suggesting that you actually go out and fail; what I'm saying is that in order to innovate you have to take risks and risks bring opportunities for increased failure. But with that failure comes the opportunity to learn. Look at successful entrepreneurs such as those on the BBC programme "Dragons' Den". Most if not all of them have failed at some point. It was past failure that actually drove them on to the success they now enjoy. And failures don't have to be massive. Perhaps you implement a solution and not all of it works. Well, don't worry; you've learned what did and didn't work and next time you can make it better.

I get challenged a lot about the issue of failure. "Surely, Jonathan," people say, "failure can't be a good thing? I mean, if we failed then we'd all be out of business."

This isn't necessarily so.

Take a step back for a moment and think about the following list, as I'm sure some of these will apply to you. Have you ever:

- had a 100% success rate with everyone you've recruited?
- made a really bad presentation, even though you worked really hard on it?
- designed a learning or leadership intervention that just didn't work?
- thought that a technology solution would work when it didn't?
- worked hard on developing an up and coming individual, only for them to fall short of the mark?

It could be a much longer list, but I'll stop it here. Failure is all around us; we fail every day in some ways and yes, some of our failures are massive. But we need to learn from our failures (which we naturally tend to do) and move on. And if you're trying something for the first time, maybe a new tool or technique, then try it quickly and don't be afraid of failing.

As Lord Leverhulme once remarked, "I know that fifty percent of my advertising is wasted. The trouble is, I don't know which fifty percent!" You'll need to brief your senior managers so that they realise that not everything you do will lead to success. This may seem a dangerous approach but it is the truth. Better to be honest about what hasn't worked—and then change it fast—rather than trying to cover up less than excellent performance with a myriad of useless KPIs and feedback sheet data.

Conclusions

It's clear that if you're a People Professional there are enough professional and business challenges to keep you occupied for many years to come.

But in addition to these challenges you'll also need to ensure that you've developed a range of personal skills which are essential for long-term success in achieving alignment with your business and customers. Remember, above all else, solve real problems and keep it simple.

Chapter 2: Activities

Below are each of the key areas we looked at in this chapter. For each one consider how close you feel you are to doing this really well and then estimate your current position (out of ten). Use this table to plan and record your progress against these challenges. It's unlikely that you'll ever get ten out of ten in each area, but improving your performance will significantly help you on the path to alignment with your business and customers.

The challenges	Current score	Your plan and/ or progress	New score
Deliver something rather than nothing			
Talk the language of business			
Solve REAL business problems			
Be a practical polymath			
Invest in your skills			
Understand technology like a kid			
Fail fast			

3

What's your marketplace really like?

> *"If the world operates as one big market, every employee will compete with every person anywhere in the world who is capable of doing the same job. There are lots of them and many of them are hungry."*

Andy Grove
Businessman, engineer, and author
A pioneer in the semiconductor industry and former CEO of
Intel Corporation

Introduction

I didn't think that I could write a book which focuses on alignment without taking a look at the marketplace in which we, as People Professionals, operate. All too often we fail to understand just what our market has to offer and the challenges it provides. For this chapter I've taken a look at one or two key elements of the UK People Professional marketplace and the UK training market in particular (because that's my background). I've brought together some indicative figures so that you can apply the learning from this chapter to your own specific People area.

In this day and age, where competition for resources is so keen, it's even more essential that as People Professionals you really understand the market in which you operate, as understanding your market, its issues and drivers is critical to your long-term success.

This chapter provides a very swift tour to some, but by no means all, of the People Professional market and provides a number of pointers to some great research which you may want to look at in more detail depending on which People specialism happens to be your focus.

The size of the people market

I thought it would be useful to try and calculate the size of the people market. It turned out to be far more difficult than I had originally thought. For a start the market is exceptionally fragmented with specialist areas such as:

- recruitment and selection
- employment law
- data protection
- learning and development
- coaching and mentoring

And for each of those listed above there are still further sub-divisions. Learning and Development, for example, can be further split into e-learning, executive training, leadership development and so on. Although there are various publications and reports which claim to have calculated the size of a particular segment, I could not find one single statistic on the size of the market as a whole. I therefore approached the Chartered Institute of Personnel and Development (CIPD) to see if they could help and after some searching even they drew a blank. I think it's fair to say that the size of the market runs into billions of pounds; what I'm not able to say is just how many billions.

The UK training market

I decided to narrow my search a little and focus on just one segment of the market so I called David Pardo, an old friend and leading analyst of the UK training market. "Hi David," I said. "A simple question for you. How big is the UK training market?"

Silence . . .

Drawing of breath . . .

Then those most immortal of words: ". . . well, it depends . . ."

I've known David for years and know that he's a total professional, so when he says "Well, it depends" I know I'm in for a detailed explanation!

David kindly spent some time explaining just how difficult it is to size the market. There are companies who are in the business of making and selling training and we can track their size via annual financial returns submitted to Companies House. So far, so good. But the size of the market also includes the amount of money spent with **all** the training companies and there are many of those. And then there's the cost of delivering training; this is much more difficult to measure. And then there's the opportunity cost (sometimes called lost opportunity) of people attending training, which could be very high depending on their role and the manner in which the organisation decides to calculate their contribution. Phew!

And that's not the end of it either. Within the world of psychometric testing there's something called a "socially acceptable response" which is when people present themselves in a socially acceptable manner to promote themselves in a positive light, e.g. saying that they would give up their seat on a train for an elderly person (when of course we know that not many people actually do this). The same issues exist within the world of the People Professional. When asked about the amount of training an organisation offers its staff, there's always a tendency to over-exaggerate to show that the organisation is doing "the right thing" and this can have an inflationary effect on the apparent market size.

But back to the question I originally asked David . . .

- According to research by Pardo Fox (David's company), in 2011 the top fifty training companies in the UK had a combined turnover of £2.154 billion.
- In 2009 *The Inquiry into the Future for Lifelong Learning* published a report into "The Private Training Market in the UK". This report also sizes the UK training market and estimates that

there are 12,300 private training companies operating above the VAT threshold, i.e. turning over more than £68,000 (at 2009 thresholds) and that between them they create a market worth £2.95 billion.

- The *UK Employer Skills Survey 2011* suggests that total employer expenditure on training is a whopping £49 billion! This is made up of £25.8 billion on-the-job and £23.2 billion off-the-job training. As mentioned earlier, the cost of people attending and delivering the training has been included in this research and removing that amount (some £34 billion) gives a UK training market of about £15 billion.

We can see therefore that the UK training market is a difficult market to size. Whilst the amount of money spent directly by companies on training services is considerable, it pales into insignificance in terms of the overall cost of employee wages to attend the training.

According to the Office for National Statistics, the median pay for both men and women in the UK for 2011 was £26,100 per year, equivalent to almost £119 per working day (based on a standard 220 working days per year).

According to the Chartered Institute for Personnel and Development (CIPD) in their Learning and Talent Development 2012 annual survey, the median number of training days received per employee is three (based on eight hours per training day). Just taking the national median pay of £119 per working day this investment in training is £357 per employee per year. If your organisation contains a greater proportion of professional jobs (as above) the costs will of course be considerably higher.

So why am I telling you all these facts? Well, because as People Professionals you are potentially dealing with £billions of organisation costs. Not convinced? Well take the NHS, the UK's largest employer with 1.3 million staff. At three days' training per year, the total cost of this is almost £464 million **in staff costs alone**!

In a paper by Jay Bahlis, he says that, "As a rule of thumb, the total annual training costs of units that spend $1 million annually on direct formal training costs will add up to over $6 million—an average factor of six times the direct costs—once the indirect costs of support staff, overheads, equipment and lost productivity are accounted for." That's a major investment for any organisation.

We think we know what we know—but do we?

On 12th February 2002 the United States Secretary of Defense Donald Rumsfeld famously said:

> "There are known knowns; there are things we know we know. We also know there are known unknowns; that is to say we know there are some things we do not know. But there are also unknown unknowns—there are things we do not know we don't know."

This quote has been used on numerous occasions for all sorts of reasons and has been lambasted by comedians. But deep down, there are some real truths for us to learn from—such as how well do we know our own industry?

The annual CIPD survey on Learning and Talent Development reveals some interesting facts. Despite the fact I mentioned earlier that there are some 12,300 private training companies in the UK, the CIPD tells us that the learning and development practices which the survey participants felt were most effective were in-house development programmes! Of the thirteen practices they listed, formal education came tenth and external workshops eleventh.

This is hardly surprising considering that many people filling in the survey will be the very people who are developing and delivering in-house programmes. Given that fact, they are hardly likely to rate external suppliers above their own abilities!

And the world around us is changing . . . FAST!

But what does the future hold for the People Profession? Well for one thing, the business world is changing faster than ever before. The US Department of Labor estimates that today's learners will have ten to fourteen jobs by the time they are 38; one out of four workers are working for a company they've been employed by for less than a year and 50% of workers are working for a company they have been employed by for less than five years. According to former US Secretary of Education Richard Riley, the top ten in-demand jobs in 2010 did not exist in 2004. We're therefore currently preparing people for jobs that don't yet exist, using technologies that haven't been invented in order to solve problems we don't even know are problems—yet.

The book "Tough Choices or Tough Times: The Report of the New Commission on the Skills of the American Workforce" says that in 1991 within the US, fewer than 50% of jobs required highly skilled people. By 2015 more than 79% of jobs will require highly skilled people. Jobs that don't need a high degree of skills will be automated or outsourced and this means that, more than ever before, we need a workforce of smart well-educated and skilled people.

And here's a stark truth: competition for jobs is now global; it's no longer confined to the local village or city. If your people are not good enough then there's someone in China or India waiting to take their place—for less. Recent information shows that one out of every five US scientists are foreign born and now fifty-six percent of US engineering PhDs are awarded to foreign-born students. An Indian engineer costs only twenty percent of what an American engineer costs. So why would I ever want American engineers?

It's no longer about theory or technology; it's about making the best from the skills we have and the skills we have in our organisations. As People Professionals we have a massive duty (possibly even burden) to ensure that our organisations learn faster and better than ever before. As Peter Senge wrote, "In the long run, the only sustainable source of competitive advantage is your organisation's ability to learn faster than its competition."

The UK coalition government is convinced that future prosperity will come not only from managing the businesses we currently have but also by inventing and leading new industries—and boy, that takes a heck of a lot of learning. And if you think that's a bit too "blue sky" then consider the impact Silicon Valley has had on the world and you'll have some idea of what they're thinking about. Our future is about solving problems and making our businesses better, and this is the role that our profession should occupy for this year and beyond. But my passionate rhetoric will come to nothing unless we change—and change we must.

Conclusions

As you've seen in this chapter, there's a number of different ways to measure the size of the market. No matter which way you chose to look at it, as a People Professional you have the ability to impact massively on your business and that of your customers.

Unlike a banker who deals in clearly traceable and identifiable money, much of your 'spend' will go unnoticed, but you still need to know what it is!

And the world is rapidly changing. Employment practices are changing, people are becoming ever more mobile and the jobs we have today may well be carried out on a different continent by people who are only just learning about them.

Chapter 3: Activities

How much do you actually know about the size and value of your specific market or about the businesses operating within it? Perhaps you know a great deal, perhaps very little, but there is always an opportunity to know a little more.

Take some time and find out all you can about the market you operate in. Whilst not a complete list, you may want to look at some of the following:

- size and value of the market
- key businesses operating within the market
- long-term growth prospects
- regional issues, e.g. does one region/country dominate the market?
- key future trends
- threats
- opportunities

Knowing your market will greatly impact your ability to understand and achieve alignment as we work through the remaining chapters.

4

Steps For Sustainable Success

"If you do things well, do them better. Be daring, be first, be different, be just."

Anita Roddick
Businesswoman, human rights activist and environmental campaigner, best known as the founder of The Body Shop, which shaped ethical consumerism.

Introduction

It may seem strange in a book all about People Professionals to talk about sustainable success. After all, most of us have, at some point, worked for some form of business, be it large or small, and in a book like this you'd have thought I'd have banged on non-stop about all the great things that People Professionals can do for a business; about how People Professionals can upskill people, reduce costs, reduce waste and increase reach through the use of technology, skills and so on. You'd probably expect me also to extoll the virtues of social media by explaining all the things that you can now do that could never be done before . . .

But let's stop right there . . .

And take a step back . . . A long step back

And look at . . . .

What businesses really want

Over the years, as the "science" of business management has developed and matured, the focus on what a business really wants has changed somewhat.

There was a time when the sole focus of a business was the maximisation of profit; often profit made at any cost to people or the environment.

Things have changed. Businesses are more aware than ever of the environment (and not just the green tree-hugging stuff) in which they operate. Businesses realise that their focus should be far more on the sustainability of their business than anything else.

Before you shout out that sustainability is all about "being green" and therefore of little consequence or impact to People Professionals, let's stop for a moment and look at some basic truths about businesses.

Don't worry if the following few pages seem like a history lesson; all will become clear . . .

Nothing lasts forever

I guess you'll all be familiar with the Dow Jones Industrial Average which is quoted time and time again on the business news. "The Dow" was founded by Charles Dow on 26th May 1896 and represented the dollar average of stocks from leading American industries. Of these original twelve, only General Electric currently remains part of that index in its current form. The other eleven were:

- American Cotton Oil Company, a predecessor company to Bestfoods, now part of Unilever
- American Sugar Company, which became Domino Sugar in 1900, now Domino Foods, Inc.
- American Tobacco Company, broken up in a 1911 antitrust action
- Chicago Gas Company, bought by People's Gas Light in 1897, now an operating subsidiary of Integrys Energy Group

- Distilling & Cattle Feeding Company, now Millennium Chemicals, formerly a division of LyondellBasell, the latter of which recently emerged from Chapter 11 bankruptcy
- Laclede Gas Company, still in operation as the Laclede Group, Inc., removed from the Dow Jones Industrial Average in 1899
- National Lead Company, now NL Industries, removed from the Dow Jones Industrial Average in 1916
- North American Company, an electric utility holding company, broken up by the U.S. Securities and Exchange Commission (SEC) in 1946
- Tennessee Coal, Iron and Railroad Company in Birmingham, Alabama, bought by U.S. Steel in 1907; U.S. Steel was removed from the Dow Jones Industrial Average in 1991
- U.S. Leather Company, dissolved in 1952
- United States Rubber Company, changed its name to Uniroyal in 1961, merged with private B.F. Goodrich in 1986, bought by Michelin in 1990.

The purpose of giving you this information is to show that businesses, no matter how big or seemingly dominant in their chosen market, can fail or be taken over by others, but their deep-down aim is to keep going in one form or another, to survive and to sustain themselves. No company lasts forever—well, not so far anyway! In my research, I came across the little-known name of Kongo Gumi, a family owned Japanese temple builder that finally closed its doors to business in 2006. Remarkably, it had been in business for the previous 1,400 years!

This chapter is all about sustainability: the ability of a company to survive through the many twists, turns and challenges that are thrown at it. As People Professionals, it is imperative that you understand the changing nature of business and the economy and the need to support your business and customers through these times. Understanding and responding to these changes and challenges is the first and arguably most critical step towards alignment.

Sudden failure or slow death

Unlike many of the original Dow companies which have merged and morphed from their original form, there are times when businesses can fail massively, publicly and quickly or can wither away and die slowly and painfully, but neither is desirable.

One business which fell off the cliff with an almighty bump was Enron. There's enough already written about what went wrong at this energy company for me not to add unnecessarily to this. However, at the heart of the failure was the fact that they didn't set their business up for the future and unfortunately they also took down with them the accountancy firm and consultants Arthur Andersen, which was found guilty of criminal charges related to the Enron account—a rather ironic end to a company whose founder was such a stickler for honesty!

But at $63.4 billion, Enron's collapse wasn't to stand long as the 'gold medal' of corporate failure. Just over six months later, in July 2002, Worldcom collapsed with a value of $103.9 billion and in 2008, at the tipping point of the financial crisis, Lehman Brothers failed with a value of $639 billion.

But the big company collapses aren't the only ones; there are plenty of others. Here's a list of some companies you may know that are no longer with us:

- Laker Airways
- British Leyland
- Tower Records
- Allied Carpets
- Woolworth
- News of the World
- Ferranti
- DeLorean
- Claims Direct
- BCCI
- TWA
- Ilford Photo
- Habitat
- Parmalat
- Kwik Save
- Maxwell Communication Corporation

Failure to reinvent

The businesses above failed for a variety of reasons. The News of the World was overwhelmed by market forces and Ilford Photo saw their market virtually disappear overnight. Sticking with the subject of photography, no company has better defined its industry than Kodak, a business that is now fighting for its corporate life.

Kodak is best known for its photographic film products. During most of the 20th century Kodak held a dominant position in this market and by 1976 had a ninety percent market share of photographic film sales in the United States alone. But by the late 1990s, Kodak was struggling as the world moved towards digital photography. Strangely though, having invented the core technology used in digital photography, Kodak was exceptionally slow in transitioning to this medium and last made a profit in 2007. Since then, Kodak has filed for bankruptcy, decided to stop making digital cameras and is now focusing on the corporate digital imaging market.

Standing tall against the market

Kodak failed to respond to the market, whereas two other giants stood tall: IBM and Apple. The pedantic historians may disagree, but it was IBM that truly brought computing to the business and personal world. Tabulators, mainframes, client-servers, networks, printers, hard drives, computer chips, the PC . . . the list is enviable by any measure. Added to the products and services, IBM staff are no slouches, having gained five Nobel prizes among literally dozens of other top-flight awards. But it wasn't enough. Between 1991 and 1993, IBM posted net losses of nearly $16 billion. The once dominant force of the industry was in freefall and hundreds of thousands of IBMers lost their jobs as the company almost became irrelevant.

In April 1993, Lou Gerstner took over as CEO of IBM and began to craft a remarkable recovery. He worked quickly to stabilise the business, and then transformed IBM into a service provider, having shed much of the legacy manufacturing capability. The famous ThinkPad, for example, is now made and owned by Lenovo of China.

Apple is another 'stand tall' company. Having made computing cool with the Macintosh and winning legions of fans, a series of CEOs (post Steve Jobs version 1.0) virtually ruined the company with financial losses year after year. When Steve Jobs returned to Apple (Version 2.0) some people suggested that Apple had literally just days of life left in it. The rest, as they say, is history.

Standing tall against the market is no easy task. It requires the total focus and co-operation of all areas of the business and it requires the People Function to be one of the key leaders.

Standing on the cliff, with your toes well over the edge

Finally, there are the businesses that are fighting for survival right now—businesses such as Nokia, who are moving in new strategic directions and working hard to define and build their future during uncertain times.

If ever a business embodied the hallmarks of sustainability and the drive to change and survive, it's Nokia. From its creation in 1865 as a pulp mill, Nokia has made the following array of seemingly unconnected products:

- paper
- electricity
- rubber products including galoshes, gas masks and tyres
- telephone cable
- televisions
- personal computers

In 1987, Nokia introduced one of the world's first handheld phones, the Mobira Cityman 900 and again, the rest is history. But the current situation is exceptionally tough.

By 2007, Nokia was selling a staggering 436 million handsets worldwide, an undisputed number one position. Indeed I'd lay down the challenge that virtually everyone reading this book (with the exception of my two sons) has at some point owned a Nokia phone. 2007 though was also the year that Apple launched the iPhone and that was the year it all changed.

Five years on and Nokia's forty percent market share has halved. The once dominant Finnish mobile phone maker said in a trading statement in April 2012 that its mobile revenues will be about €4.2bn, a 40% year-on-year fall, which would translate to a loss of €126m (£104m). It would be the sixth quarter in a row in which Nokia's mobile operating profit has declined. The company expects no improvement in the second quarter of the trading year.

The new CEO, Stephen Elop (previously with Microsoft) is trying to stop the rot. His famous "burning platform" memo was used as a wakeup call for the company. I've put the full text of this landmark memo in Appendix A so you can see its boldness.

Nokia has decided that it does not want to go over the cliff; it wants to survive and add another illustrious chapter to its proud history. It has decided that it wants to thrive and survive; it does not want to die.

The strangeness of change

For a bit of fun, here are a number of products, none of which we'd really consider necessary, or indeed politically correct today, but which were once deemed to be perfectly "normal" many years ago:

- the wig iron
- the motorcyclist's pipe
- steering wheel heaters
- gold coin changers—that's right, put in your money and get a gold coin in return
- double cigarette holders
- skirt lifters—I kid you not!
- hand-operated windscreen wipers

Fashion and fad; they all come and go. Over the years, what was once seen as the norm is now seen in a very different light. Not that many years ago, some of the following would have been seen as more than acceptable in a day-to-day working context:

- smoking at work—not outside in a designated smokers' cabin but actually at your desk
- drinking at lunchtime—the classic 'liquid lunch'.

I mention this because all things change. People change, fashions change, tastes change. Only the other day I listened to a podcast which talked about the introduction of avocado pears into the UK. According to the podcast there was the need to have trained people on hand to tell you how to use this new product as well as beautifully printed fliers to encourage you to use avocados for dinner parties. How times have changed!

We've seen that all things change and that while some companies thrive and survive others will wither and die. As People Professionals, you need to know the key ingredients to deliver a sustainable business and we'll now look at these in more detail.

The three pillars of sustainability

People can argue about all the various ingredients for business sustainability and suggest a number of "golden rules" but true business sustainability boils down to just three key principles or pillars. These are:

- people
- profit
- planet

Let's look at each of these in more detail.

People

"Fantastic," I hear you all cry, "it's about bloody time he talked a bit more about people!"

It almost goes without saying that in order for any business to flourish and survive it must attract, develop and retain the very best people it can. Not only that, it must look after those people, reward them, give them meaningful roles and tasks and help them nurture their talent. Wow, this is just the sort of stuff that we People Professionals do—how wonderful is that!

But before you shout "hurrah" and put down this book thinking you've got all the answers, take a moment to think about the earlier sections of this chapter. Companies have failed because people did not do the right things (Enron), or did not react to the market in the right way (Kodak), or took their eye off the ball (Apple). People cannot only make a business; they can also break a business—and fast.

People Professionals and the People Function already play a critical role in attracting, selecting, inducting (orientating or on-boarding), training, nurturing and of course firing people. But acting out a process is not going to be enough. If you want to be truly aligned—and of course you do—then you need to have a clear insight into the direction your business and customers are heading.

As you read earlier, IBM transformed itself on a number of fronts. It shed virtually all its manufacturing and 'low value' capabilities and moved into the 'higher value' consulting and services areas. The challenges that IBM faced during these times were immense and for the People Function there was a major opportunity to shine, an opportunity to lead with:

- retaining key people
- retraining for new roles
- letting people go—with dignity
- managing the change
- communication

- people transformation (posh words for turning people around and pointing them in the right direction)
- strategic alignment—it's no longer about just being a technology company

People Professionals are naturally "people people" and generally understand the "softer" side of the business. That's great, but you need to realise that people on their own are never enough. Businesses need to ensure that the people they employ (and this includes you) do more than turn up on a daily basis and collect a pay cheque.

People Professionals in companies that will survive need to demonstrate a particular set of skills. They need to work well beyond their current operational bubble and reach out into new territories. Peter Fisk's book, "People, Planet, Profit" described the five characteristics (the five Cs) for 21st century leaders, which really struck a chord with me as I could immediately see the impact for People Professions. Peter's Five Cs are:

> **Communicator:** someone who articulates the vision and provides an inspiring direction for the business. Someone who lives and readily extols the values and personality of their business' brand. Externally they are ambassadors, engaging stakeholders and being the human face of the business.

> **Connector:** someone who brings the best people and ideas together. This isn't someone who's got a million friends on Facebook or who shouts non-stop on Twitter; this is someone who's well-connected both inside and outside the organisation and who has a wide range of connections, not just those in the People Profession. These people are classic Belbin Resource Investigators!

> **Catalyst:** someone who adores change, who seeks it out as a friend, who looks for new possibilities. This is someone who's at the hub of driving change. They push the business to innovate and deliver with positive impact.

> **Coach:** someone who works with and supports people at all levels across the business. This person works across a number

of businesses, sharing their knowledge, experience, insights and instincts.

Conscience: someone who knows what's right and wrong, who understands and abides by a set of business ethics and who challenges others to do the same.

Take a good, long, hard look at the above five characteristics. Do you, as a People Professional, possess these traits? If you do, are you adequately demonstrating these to your business and customers?

Profit

The second sustainability pillar is profit, a dirty word for some and potentially an alien word to many People Professionals!

I say "an alien word" because within the People "world" most of what we deal with on a day-to-day basis is cost, not profit. Here's some proof: how many of you regularly hear these statements:

- "How much does that cost?"
- "How much does it cost to recruit someone?"
- "Can't you get more people on that course?"
- "Do you realise what this training/development is costing us?"
- "Do we really need to pay £x to coach them in something they already do?"
- "Your department cost us £x last year."

Each of the above statements—and there could have been many more—deals with the issue of cost. People Professionals seemingly always have to cut costs, justify costs and manage with ever smaller budgets. It's the world we live in and the world we're used to.

And of course cost **is** important; businesses need to keep their costs under control, they need to spend wisely and they need to strike great deals. Cost containment is necessary to drive profit and profit is what gives a business options for the future. But as I said earlier, businesses now realise that although profit is necessary for survival it's not about profit at any cost.

Profit is a necessity for all businesses. I realise that year one MBA students and those who run businesses (I've been both, and am still the latter) will shout "It's not about profit, it's about cash flow", but bear with me on this . . .

Make no mistake, profit is a driver for all businesses and not just those in the private sector. Put simply, profit is the difference between your income and the costs of providing your service. Profit is necessary for business growth, for investment and to provide funds for a rainy day.

Let's make sure I say this loud and clear . . .

Profit is **NOT** a dirty word.

People Professionals need to do all they can to understand the profit motives within their own business. I'm often challenged that the profit motive doesn't apply within charities (the third sector) and I always argue back with a vengeance. Even for charities profit is necessary to sustain their business. Remember, it's the difference between your income and the costs of providing your service. For charities that's the difference between the money they raise and the cost of raising that money. It's no use if every £100 of money raised costs a charity £99, because there's little left for those who need it! Charities, like all businesses, must keep a close eye on the costs to ensure they have the greatest amount of money available to help them grow and thrive.

I realise that at times this book may seem 'a bit too businessy', a 'bit too hard' or 'a bit too far removed' from general People books; but there's a real reason for this. Over the years, I've spoken at many conferences aimed squarely at the People Professional and it's become blindingly obvious that relatively few People Professionals actually understand the basics of business or profit dynamics. They seem to have this rather misguided view that the money they need for their activities will miraculously appear just because they've asked for it. And that's not meant as a criticism, it's a fact.

So to recap my simple model of profit:

$$\text{Profit} = \text{Revenue} - \text{Cost}$$

Although the above equation is factually correct, you also need to understand:

- what **contributes** to, and **impacts** on your profit
- what **drives** profit within your business
- what makes the really **big** difference.

You'll also need to be able and prepared to talk about these with your colleagues and senior managers. Let's now put the above into some sort of context.

At the time of writing we're just a few days away from the opening ceremony of the London 2012 Olympic Games. Security company G4S has been awarded a £284 million contract to supply 13,700 security guards for the duration of the games. Unfortunately, despite the date for the Games being known **seven** years in advance **and** the contract being awarded in plenty of time, G4S failed to recruit the required number of security guards, the gap being provided by the UK Army and other military personnel. This failure has cost G4S between thirty and fifty million pounds on the current contract, not to mention the public embarrassment and humiliation and the business repercussions that are sure to come later.

Now, if ever there's a situation that falls squarely at the door of the People Professional, it's this one! Sadly, the head of G4S claimed that he didn't know about the situation until literally days before the Games and naturally some heads had to roll. But for a People Professional this should have been a 'bread and butter' assignment. After all, it was about:

- recruitment
- selection
- training, and
- deployment

And yet despite this—total failure!

But hang on a minute, you may cry, how on earth could People Professionals have helped avoid the G4S problem? Simple—by engaging with the business, understanding risks and working with the leadership to mitigate those risks on an ongoing basis. The truth is that most People Professionals just don't know what the critical issues are within their business or seem oblivious to those that get waved in their faces. Here's a real example . . .

I often hear people at conferences moaning that they've got to work on developing and delivering "boring" compliance training. I always say the same thing: if you think compliance is boring, imagine the excitement when it all goes wrong! Joking aside, many corporate failures and near-failures have been caused by massive non-compliance. Here are some examples:

Piper Alpha:	Failure of the permit to work system. 167 lives lost.
Chernobyl:	Failure to prepare and follow procedures. 47 lives lost with countless more affected.
Texas City:	Failure in equipment, risk management, staff management, working culture at the site, maintenance and inspection. 15 lives lost.
Deepwater Horizon:	Multiple failures to secure the wellhead, failures of the blow out preventer. 11 lives lost.
Banking crisis:	Failure to manage and monitor an entire industry. Enough said!

I've purposefully kept the above examples overly simple, however for People Professionals the issue of compliance can be an **excellent** way to demonstrate value to your business and ensure that you've done all the right things to ensure the long-term success and sustainability for your business.

Here's a little teaser for you. Most of you will, at some point, have taken a flight from place A to place B. We all love to hate airlines but if you had to list just **two** critical roles which, if they failed to work properly, would bring an airline to its knees, what roles would they be? Here's a few I suspect you're thinking about:

- pilots
- air traffic control
- check in desk operators
- transport to the aeroplane
- maintenance teams
- safety inspectors.

But want to know the two most critical roles? Here you go:

- baggage handlers
- fuel buyers

Now I suspect that many of you got the first one (baggage handlers) but did you **honestly** get the second? Clearly with the best maintenance, pilots, check-in crew etc. in the world, if the bags aren't loaded on the plane then it's not going anywhere. The fuel buyer is also critical to success. If they buy the fuel at too high a price then every passenger loaded onto a plane will effectively be financially bleeding it dry.

As with all my stories in this book, there is a clear purpose and meaning. For many People Professionals their primary focus will be profit creation by "making people better" or "making them sell more" or whatever the performance issue of the day is. But profit is not just about making more sales or containing cost. Long-term success comes about because profit is maintained and protected year after year. The People Function has a key role to play in helping to protect long-term profit by working with the business to prevent the sort of disasters that can bring a business to its knees.

Planet

The final sustainability pillar is the planet, i.e. as a result of operating your business, what's the effect you have on the planet in terms of impact, resources used, waste generated and so on?

I have to declare up-front that I'm not a 'green' or a 'tree hugger'. However, it's worth realising that as competition intensifies, businesses are struggling to do more and more with less and less. There's a real passion in some businesses to reduce the amount of material it takes to make their product and this will only increase.

One recent challenge I saw asked businesses how they would go about running their current operation with twenty percent less—**of everything.** That's fewer staff, lower power consumption, less CO_2 emitted and so on. Don't think it's a challenge? Try working out how you would survive next year with a twenty percent reduction in your income. It's a challenging time!

And I mention this not because it's current headline news, but because it **will** become business as usual. As People Professionals, you **will** be challenged with helping your business and customers do more with less and some of you may already be rising to this challenge. If you can do this well, you will thrive and prosper. If you're unable to make the change then you'll be marginalised.

Various reports—some doom-laden—set out challenges for the future and identify key resources that will dominate the ability of organisations (and indeed civilisations) to flourish. These resources are so central to our very survival that it's possible we may actually go to war over them. What most agree on is that there are four critical resources to our survival in twenty years' time. These are:

- water

- food
- energy
- climate

That's it. Four simple things that we may actually go to war over! Not convinced? Then how hard would **you** fight to make sure you and your family had something to drink, or a place to live that wasn't impacted by floods, earthquakes or tornadoes? And with that in mind, how would you begin to support your business and your customers to use, say, twenty percent less water? What new challenges would that bring and how would you overcome them?

And helping your business or customers use twenty percent less water sounds OK—doesn't it? I mean, we don't use that much water anyway, do we? But perhaps we do.

Here are the shocking facts. It takes:

- 39,000 gallons of water to make a car
- 62,000 gallons of water to make a ton of steel
- 518 gallons of water to make just one car tyre
- 1,800 gallons of water just to grow the cotton to make you a pair of jeans over 520 gallons of water to make a hamburger
- 400 gallons of water to grow the cotton to make your t-shirt
- 1,500 gallons of water to make a barrel of beer—that's almost six pints of water for every pint of beer
- And it even takes 53 gallons of water to make your favourite takeaway latte!

That's right, 53 gallons of water to make a latte! It seems beyond reason, but then you've had to grow the coffee (and potentially the sugar), you've had to make a plastic lid, a cardboard cup and a small cardboard sleeve, oh and you've had to pour water over the coffee itself!

But it gets even worse. That glass of wine you enjoy with your evening meal . . . that's another 58 gallons of water just there!

But water isn't the only challenge that organisations face. It's estimated that at current levels of consumption we have only:

- 18 years of lead remaining
- 20 years of tin
- 25 years of copper
- 64 years of iron ore, and
- 69 years of aluminium.

So what are we learning here? Well, what we know is that in the future the ability of an organisation to thrive **may** depend on its ability to access, control and reduce the amount of raw materials it uses. But so what? I mean, no one actually bothers about this at the moment, do they?

Let's stop for a moment and think. If, as People Professionals, our business is trying to do more with less or trying to reduce waste and consumption, then shouldn't you also do the same?

For example, do you know the carbon footprint of someone attending an interview with your business or for an employee to attend an internal training course? Do you do all you can to reduce your use of paper, increase recycling etc?

Doing more with less is not something solely for others; it is something for all of us and we must rise to the challenge for if we don't then we are out of step and therefore out of alignment with the rest of our business and our customers.

One recent example of the immense effort needed to do more with less is the desire for Tata motors to develop a car for the Indian market with the unbelievably low price (to us in the western world) of $2,100. Just think for a moment: how on earth can you produce a car with a price tag that low?

As People Professionals, what do you think would help reduce the costs of a car? I appreciate you're not necessarily engineers, but have a think anyway; challenge yourself. After all, as you saw in earlier chapters, the pressure on our profession to do more with less is increasing enormously, so go on, give it a go!

The ten ways I would reduce the cost of building a car would be . . .

1.

2.

3.

4.

5.

6.

7.

8.

9.

10.

Here are some of the ways that the Nano's designers implemented many of their cost-reducing measures. Perhaps you came up with some of these too.

- The boot is only accessible from inside the car, saving steel, hinges and latches.
- One windscreen wiper instead of the usual pair.
- No power steering; it's unnecessary due to its light weight.
- Three lug nuts on the wheels instead of the usual four (saving 25%).
- Only one wing mirror.
- No radio or CD player fitted as standard.
- No airbags on any model.
- The 624cc rear engine has only two cylinders and is therefore very small.
- No air conditioning on the base model.

So far, so good? We've looked at the issues of sustainability, but there are also a number of other issues that constantly provide key challenges to any business and if you, as People Professionals, can have a positive impact on them this will really demonstrate an understanding and alignment to your business and customers. Let's look at these in more detail.

Six key challenges

As well as the various issues I've introduced you to in this chapter, I believe there are six key challenges which can fundamentally impact on the success or otherwise of almost every business. Anything you can do which has a positive impact on these challenges **will** bring substantial rewards. The six key challenges are:

- cycle time
- time shifting
- logistical costs
- reskilling
- speed of delivery
- convenience

Let's look at these challenges in more detail:

1. **Cycle time**—this is the time taken to achieve **anything** within your business. While speed to market and the first mover advantage is massively critical to any business, for People Professionals having a positive impact on cycle time can be as simple as reducing the time it takes to develop a new learning or leadership intervention or simply reducing the time taken to recruit a new member of staff. Reducing cycle time will **always** be of advantage to your business or customers.

2. **Time shifting**—let's be brutally honest, nine to five working is no longer the norm, especially as the global economy expands and ever smarter forms of mobile communications continue to grow. Remember those days when you could look at your desk and say "All done!" Well, no longer! As the working day expands to meet the demands of business, so the personal impact on all of us grows, often with detrimental results. People Professionals have a vital role to play in managing the working day and ensuring that employees are not only making the very best of the 24/7/365 world in which we now live, but do so in a constructive and lasting manner.

3. **Logistical costs**—these are the physical costs of being in and operating a business and include such things as employee costs, rent, rates, distribution costs, IT costs and so on. Every business—and yes, I do mean **every** business—is seeking to reduce these costs wherever possible. For some businesses basic logistical costs can be almost crippling. According to the UK Road Transport Association, the cost of the fuel and a driver accounts for 39% of the overall cost of operating a large articulated lorry. All it takes is a small rise in the cost of fuel and many hauliers could be facing ruin. Even for the seemingly heady heights of UK Premiership football, some of the logistical costs beggar belief. Manchester United, which, according to *TalkSport*, is the most popular football club in the world with an estimated 354 million fans, spends 46% of its £331 million income on wages. This, however, pales into insignificance compared with Chelsea, the fourth most

popular club, which spends an eye-watering 85% of all its income on wages. This is nothing, however, if we add Manchester City, the 11th most popular club in the world, to the mix. Manchester City spends a staggering 114% of its income on wages. That's right, it actually spends **more** money than it earns—well that's a rich owner for you! On a more down-to-earth point, businesses are constantly looking to remove operating costs. Less waste, tighter salaries, less travel, less money spent on training and L&D and HR and so on. Although you may not want to cut costs from your own budgets, showing that you are able to do more with less, or at least accomplish the same with less, will be well received within any business.

4. **Reskilling**—although this is self-explanatory, it's another massive issue for businesses. But it's not always about new software or the latest management techniques. In today's business world, the level of compliance that's needed to stay the right side of the law increases yearly. Just keeping up is a major task and it's an even bigger issue if your business is in a heavily regulated environment such as finance, healthcare, oil, gas or nuclear. For all businesses the cost of keeping the workforce up-to-date or even staying in front with legislation is considerable. As People Professionals your business and your customers **will** look to you to tackle the reskilling issue. No longer is a mass-classroom-sheep-dip approach always appropriate (or affordable), so you'll need to be creative in your approach and executions to ensure skills are maintained with minimal impact on the financial or operational areas of the business.

5. **Speed of delivery**—this is the amount of time it takes to deliver a product or service. (To reiterate, the time to make the product or service is the cycle time.) For a business like Amazon, speed of delivery is literally what you'd think it is—the time it takes to get your order to your front door from the moment you decide to purchase something. For People Professionals the speed of delivery is very much about how quickly you can deliver your products or services to your business or customer. As businesses constantly seek to streamline their processes, so the speed of

delivery of **everything** increases. Businesses can't afford to wait weeks for computer equipment, or training courses, or new staff; they want it all yesterday, or even quicker if possible!

6. **Convenience**—in the hugely consumer-based society of the twenty-first century convenience is exceptionally high on all of our priority lists. We want products and services at a time and place to suit our needs. We now want banking on a 24/7/365 basis, via branches, the telephone, internet and mobile phones. For People Professionals the challenges are the same. When airline company British Airways introduced its self-service HR system it saved itself over £150 million per year in processing costs and had much happier staff; staff who could book their own holidays, make charitable donations from their salary and generally manage their own affairs. And the real success, the convenience of staff to carry out transactions with their employer at a time and place to **suit them**. As People Professionals we need to ensure that convenience outweighs process so that the customers and people in our business can readily and easily access our services. Convenience is about speed, simplicity and making sure that the process doesn't get in the way of the desired result.

Conclusions

Let's recap on what sustainable success has to do with alignment. It's simple: if you fail to understand and address the challenges of your business or customer then you fail them completely. There's no middle ground, no almost right solution, no nearly there path to success. If you don't understand and address the challenges of your business or customer at a deep level then you cannot serve them, cannot add value and cannot help them to survive.

As I've shown in this chapter, businesses have a wide range of challenges they need to overcome in order to survive and flourish. The role of the People Professional is to make sure that businesses can achieve the goals to which they aspire and make the changes necessary for success. Will the

People Function always be the centre of activity? Of course not; however it should be the focal point for many of the activities that you've just read about, because if it's not then it's certainly not getting close to being aligned!

Chapter 4: Activities

Use the following activities to draw together the key learning from this chapter.

You may not have all the information readily to hand to answer these questions, but if you don't then this will tell you something anyway. So let's see what you know about the following:

- What challenges is your business or that of a key customer facing, both now and within the next three to five years?
- As a People Professional, what can you do to help with these challenges?
- How much did you cost your business or your customers last year? That's salaries, expenses, delivery of services, consultants—the lot!
- What would you do if you had to cut your department/function budgets or your fees by twenty percent within the next year?
- Taking each of the six key drivers discussed in this chapter, what would you do to improve them for your business or a customer?

5

The Recipe For Business Success

"The trouble with organizing a thing is that pretty soon folks get to paying more attention to the organization than to what they're organized for."

Laura Ingalls Wilder
Author who wrote the *Little House* series of books based on her childhood in a pioneer family.

Introduction

A recurring theme that's often held against the People Profession is that they don't understand business and what it is, how it works and what makes it tick. I'll echo those themes, because if I didn't then there would be little point for this book! However, as I've touched on a number of times already, People Professionals all too often stray away from "business issues" as though they are some form of impenetrable barrier beyond which they cannot go. This should not be the case. People Professionals should not just be familiar with understanding business, they should also be totally comfortable with the way a business operates.

In this chapter, I'll begin exploring some of the key building blocks for a successful business so that you thoroughly understand the components and can begin to replicate these in your own field.

There must be a recipe

These days it's all about being fast-paced, about doing things quickly, about getting things done and moving on. We're forever reading about "get rich quick schemes" or "double your money in twenty days" or "I can make you a millionaire" or "ten easy steps to . . . just about anything".

And it's the same with business, isn't it? Surely it must be! After all, virtually every successful business has been examined in minute detail to determine what makes it special and stand out from the crowd. Here are some examples:

Company	Success Criteria
IBM	Scale, processes, reach, market dominance and legendary customer service. IBM ensured that all the pieces worked together—a truly integrated company.
Walmart	Successful because of the way it used IT and logistics to drive down prices. Because it was family owned it also took a longer-term view of issues.
Dell	Success was mass customisation and putting the customer in charge of the ordering process, oh, and direct selling.
Sony	Miniaturisation—who can forget the impact of the Walkman and the radically small first generation VAIOs?
Apple	What else but fantastically cool design and easy to use products—oh, and a superb ecosystem with the App Store, iTunes and iCloud.
Nordstrom	Fantastic customer service—one of the first and still a leader.

I could go on, but there's no point. For every successful company there are people trying to find the single unique success factor, but it's not there. It never will be. There's no one single factor that, if copied, will ensure success for your organisation. Many computer companies have tried to replicate the 'Dell way', but none have really thrived. No one company can really come close to Apple for being 'cool' (let alone for innovation), even though many have tried and even the might of Google has (so far) failed to dent the social media juggernaut that is Facebook. A single factor is just not enough; it never is. You cannot merely copy or imitate and you can't fabricate something out of nothing.

Long before chemistry was a science, there was alchemy. One of the supreme quests of alchemy was to turn lead into gold, thereby fabricating 'something' out of 'nothing'. In short, it is possible but it requires a vast input of energy, such that the overall cost of turning lead into gold greatly outweighs the value of the resulting gold. In short, a recipe that doesn't really work.

But what exactly is a recipe, and is it possible to work out what makes a business successful—to identify its recipe—no matter what field that business is in?

One definition of recipe is "a formula for, or means to, a desired end: *a recipe for success.*"

What if it **was** possible to unearth the recipe for a successful business? I mean, just imagine how valuable that would be to actually know which recipe made a difference? And if you knew what a successful recipe looked like then surely you could begin to look at how that recipe applied within your business or that of your customers. Then you could try and replicate or support it, and before long you'd not only be more successful but you'd have truly aligned to the success of your business. Now how good would that be?

But let's stand back for a moment . . . understanding a recipe for success is just one part of the overall alignment equation. Not only do you need to understand what makes a business a success, but you also need to ensure that you offer adequate and timely support for your business in these vital areas and by doing so you will be well on the way to achieving alignment.

The recipe I'll introduce you to is not just any old "I think that XYZ makes a successful business"; it's a recipe that is well researched and backed up with hard data. Here's the chance to understand what makes a great business tick and the opportunity to develop the recipe to help you in your quest for alignment. Excited? Then let's go!

Basic nuts and bolts

Over the years there's been a plethora of books telling us why various companies were successful but these were largely based on a single dominant feature, some of which I've mentioned earlier. The truth is that just as a recipe is made up of a number of ingredients, so it is with business success. It is **never** about a single ingredient, but about a number of ingredients that are well-balanced and mixed together in the right way.

But although there are many 'Here's a recipe' books available, there are relatively few that are built upon the foundation of strong research and analysis. One book that is backed up by research (if you're really into book reading) is *Beyond Performance* by Scott Keller and Colin Price. This is a very well put together book which clearly demonstrates the link between the 'five frames of performance and health' and overall business performance.

Keller and Price outline the "Five Frames" as being:

Aspire:	Where do you want to go?
Assess:	How ready are you to go there?
Architect:	What do you need to do to get there?
Act:	How do you manage your journey?
Advance:	How do you keep moving forward?

You may also have come across the McKinsey 7S Framework, which also provides a recipe for success under the headings:

Structure:	What's the overall structure of your organisation?
Strategy:	What strategy have you decided upon?
Systems:	What systems (IT and others) do you have to enable success?
Skills:	What skills do you have, and what do you need?
Style:	What's the style of the organisation—loose/tight etc.?
Staff:	What staff do you have and are they the right ones?
Shared values:	What are your values and are they shared by everybody?

Both of the above are excellent frameworks. However, to achieve a really good alignment with your business I wanted something a little more specific so I've used the ground-breaking book published in 2003 called "What Really Works" by William Joyce, Nitin Nohria and Bruce Roberson. For many years I've referenced this book in my professional career and have returned to it time and time again for guidance and inspiration. Harvard Business Review said of this book, "Forget the fads, here are the basic, proven building blocks of long-term company success." Wow—that's good enough for me!

But before I get into the details, and there are a lot of these, let's take a moment to see why the key issues mentioned in "What Really Works" actually make a difference to a business.

According to the work carried out to write the book "What Really Works" there's an almost unique equation which summarises the success of organisations. The equation is:

$$4 + 2$$

It doesn't look much, does it? It doesn't feel as balanced and beautiful as Einstein's

$E = MC^2$ and it certainly doesn't look as sexy and complex as a Fourier series:

$$f(x) = a_0 + \sum_{n=1}^{\infty} \left(a_n \cos\frac{n\pi x}{L} + b_n \sin\frac{n\pi x}{L} \right)$$

But 4 + 2 is a fundamental building block of business success and is based on:

Four core areas which are:

- strategy
- execution
- culture
- structurew

And **two areas** taken from:

- leadership
- talent
- mergers and partnerships
- innovation

As a People Professional and having read the last list, you'll probably be jumping up and down screaming that leadership and/or talent should be included in the core areas. After all, they are **so** important to success that who on earth could possibly 'demote' them to 'pick two from four in the second division'—shock horror!

But get this . . .

Despite what you may think, People Professionals are NOT always at the centre of success in your business,
so get over it!

I'm being provocative to make a point because although talent and leadership are clearly important within a business their place in building a truly successful business will depend on the type of business and the environment in which it operates. I'll look at these areas in more detail later, but for now let's move on and look at each of the key areas and how these apply to our profession. It's worth noting that the results from the original research showed that businesses that applied the 4 + 2 model showed a:

- 945% return to shareholders (normal organisations achieve 62% returns)
- 415% increase in sales (compared to 83% for normal companies)
- 358% increase in assets (versus 97%), and
- 326% increase in operating income (as against 22% for normal companies)

So by any measure of business success, if applied correctly (as we shall see later) these key issues **will** deliver positive and lasting benefits.

But again, as throughout this book, you may be wondering why on earth you need to understand these issues. The answer is quite simple:

A failure to understand business . . .
is a failure!

By all means buy a copy of the book to read and learn about the intimate details of the studies the authors carried out. However, for the purpose of where we're heading, I've concentrated the key messages into a few pages to focus your approaches to alignment.

Make no mistake, this is **really** hot stuff. If you understand the success recipe of an organisation then it's possible for you to understand and apply the recipe to your own business. And surprise, surprise, if you're a success then your business will think a whole lot more of what you offer and you'll have a much higher chance of gaining the alignment you're seeking.

So without further ado, let's move on and look at each of the key areas and begin to understand how they apply the lessons from each one to your profession.

Conclusions

It's critically important for People Professionals to understand that businesses have tried for many years to replicate the success of key players in the market. However, time and again they have found that what they thought was the special ingredient for one business just doesn't work so well, if at all, in others.

Research has now shown that rather than having a magical "silver bullet", businesses are successful because they use a set of fundamental building blocks, each of which contributes to long-term success. As People Professionals, knowledge of these building blocks will help you to understand better your business and the contribution you need to make it a success.

Chapter 5: Activities

This is a particularly short chapter as we're about to delve into the details of what makes the 4 + 2 recipe a success for businesses.

But before we do, it would be useful for you to think about your own business or that of your customers and consider the following questions:

1. What do you think makes your business (or that of your customers) successful? List as many elements as you can. Examples could include great customer service, innovative products, value for money, logistics etc.
2. For each of the elements you've identified, think of **three** ways you could help improve that element even more. For example, if great customer service was an element you chose, then think of three ways you could make it even better.
3. Think about the **two** closest competitors to your business (or your customers'). What do they have that you don't? What could you learn from them?

6

Strategy

"However beautiful the strategy, you should occasionally look at the results."

Winston Churchill
Politician and statesman known for his leadership of the
United Kingdom during the Second World War

Introduction

If ever you want to see fear in the eyes of a manager from our profession then simply ask them about strategy! Of course this won't apply to all managers, but for many years it's been my experience that although managers can be excellent at ensuring operational issues are handled well, they tend to look very nervous when the 'strategy' word is mentioned!

In the last chapter I briefly introduced you to the 4 + 2 model as a recipe for business success. In this chapter I'll be taking a look at the first of the four core areas—strategy—and explaining the key issues necessary not only to better understand strategy and its effect, but also, as a result, to better understand how to develop a great strategy yourself and how this helps you align what you do to the needs of your business.

There's a strategy for everything

I suspect that for many of you reading this book, strategies could well be 'things' generated by others for you to implement. Understanding strategy allows you to gain better control of your own destiny (and that of your area/department) and truly align your skills to the success of the business. But first, a little history . . .

Strategy originates from the military and refers to a plan of action designed to achieve a particular goal. Strategy has been extended beyond its traditional arena, military and grand strategy, to business, economics, game theory and other fields.

In many businesses, strategy is viewed as a process for determining where the business is going over the next year or, more typically, the next three to five years. Some businesses will extend their strategy to twenty years and I've even heard of one company that was looking forward 250 years!

It's impossible to cover all aspects of strategy within this book; after all, some people spend years at business school learning the theory, so to move you forward I've focused on the key issues which I've used with success over the years, and I've distilled these into easily digestible chunks which are of best use to People Professionals.

As I've mentioned, from all the reading I've done over the years and the numerous conferences I've attended, it's fair to say that strategy isn't something particularly well understood by People Professionals. Of course they talk about strategy, but primarily only when combined to form:

- informal learning strategies
- recruitment strategies
- content strategies
- e-learning strategies
- talent development strategies
- social media strategies
- content curation strategies
- mobile learning strategies
- learning technologies strategy

In fact, you can put almost any set of People Professional buzz words in front of 'strategy' and say it's done! Here's proof . . .

- business partner strategy

- employee engagement strategy
- reward and recognition strategy
- employment law strategy
- learning and development strategy
- change management strategy
- coaching and mentoring strategy
- discipline and grievance strategy
- absence strategy age discrimination strategy

OK, OK. Enough is enough, but hopefully you get the idea. The problem is that the 'strategy' word has been so overdone as to be virtually meaningless, but as People Professionals you **really** need to understand business strategy, because if you don't then you'll never achieve alignment—and now's a really good time to start!

Knowing your business strategy first

I've had the pleasure of working with a wide range of businesses over the years, helping them develop their strategies for the challenges they face. Whenever I've begun work with a People Function within a large business I've always started with basically the same question: "What's the strategy for your business?"

It's a simple enough question. However, like so many simple questions there's rarely a simple answer. Often I'll be told, "Don't worry about that, Jonathan, let's just develop our strategy and take it from there." But of course we can't just do that. If we did then we'd be failing to align within the business and therefore anything we developed would be no more than some random guess—hardly a professional approach. As you can imagine, there's little use developing your strategy without first understanding the strategy of your business.

According to a white paper entitled "Navigating the Perfect Storm in L&D" by the Learning and Performance Institute, although 81% of L&D professionals surveyed by the LPI claimed that their organisation had a learning strategy, LPI accreditations indicate that many of these strategies are actually little more than one-year operating plans.

In-year operational plans are **not** the same as a strategy. Let's therefore look at what makes a great strategy and the importance of strategy in achieving alignment.

The five strategy rules

In the last chapter we looked at the recipe for business success and just as a business can potentially have a success recipe, so can a strategy; in this case there are five rules for a successful strategy. As with all rules, merely following them is not enough; you've got to work hard and make them come alive in order to stand a chance of achieving alignment.

The five strategy rules are:

1. starting from the outside in
2. keep growing and supporting the core business
3. clear value propositions for the customer
4. fine tune for the marketplace
5. communicate clearly with stakeholder groups

Let's look at each of the rules in turn and expand on what they mean to you.

Rule 1: Starting from the outside in

Many of the People Professional strategies I've heard about, seen and experienced all tend to be rather insular—they are about how individuals or departments can achieve what they want, rather than understanding what the business requires and organising a suitable response.

I know this only too well as I speak from experience in this matter. When I had no grey hairs (and that's a **long** time ago), I pursued the path of putting my own needs and wants temporarily before those of the business.

Many of the strategies I see are more often than not developed the wrong way round, i.e. from the inside out: focusing more on the "inside" issues of your department or your skillset or your focus areas rather than those of the business. The problem is that "inside out" strategies read something like this:

> "Learning and development needs to be an integral part of our practice and culture. It should be available to all, flexible to suit different learning styles and work patterns. It should meet the needs of the individual, the team and the organisation, both now and in the future."

Bolton NHS Primary Care Trust Learning & Development Strategy, 2008-2010

Yuck!

The above statement was point number one in a list of nine key summary points of the strategy. Not one of the nine summary points mentioned a business issue—they were **all** "inside out" issues focusing on areas such as appraisals, learning management systems, encouraging team learning and user-friendly process paperwork.

An honest question: on a scale of one to five (where five is good), how aligned do you really think the above statement is to the needs of the business?

And that's the first problem; we have a tendency to focus on 'our' needs rather than those of the business. Of course appraisals are important and have their place, but for me that's all about 'business as usual' rather than solving a real business issue.

We must learn to put the needs of our business first—always.

An "outside in" strategy is totally different. It starts with the needs of the business on the "outside" and then proceeds to explain how these will be met—the "inside".

Here's another example taken from the Natural History Museum Learning and Development Strategy 2007:

> "Strategic Aim 1—to equip employees with the skills needed to deliver the corporate plan and Museum brand values and qualities
>
> We will do this by:
>
> • Ensuring that our approach to Learning and Development identification and analysis begins with the linkage of objectives to corporate and departmental plans . . .
> • Designing events and programmes relevant to corporate plan priorities"

I love this! Listen to those wonderful words ringing out: "**deliver the corporate plan**", "**linkage of objectives to corporate and departmental plans**" and "**events and programmes relevant to corporate plan priorities**". Sheer strategy poetry!

And on a scale of one to five (where five is good), how aligned do you think the above statement is to the needs of the business? Are you starting to see the difference?

The Natural History Museum Learning and Development Strategy puts the business first—the "outside"—and then works towards explaining how it will all be delivered—the "inside". Professionally, it's a whole lot easier to sell a strategy that starts with the business rather than starting with some "pink and fluffy" statement about being "flexible to suit different learning styles" approach.

Starting from the outside in achieves many things:

• it ensures you focus on the needs of the business
• it delivers strategies that will be recognised and supported
• it's more likely to gain appropriate funding and resources
• it's aligned!

Rule 2: Keep growing and supporting the core business

Every business, no matter how big or small, has an element of core business. This isn't the same as core capability; it's even simpler than that. A fish and chip shop (for example) may cater for the odd party or small event, but at its heart it's still a fish and chip shop. It's not a fancy five-star restaurant, it'll be open late on a Saturday evening and it'll wrap your meal in paper. It understands what it is, who its customers are and what they expect.

General Electric (GE) is one of the most admired business organisations in the world. GE operates through four core businesses, which are:

- energy
- technology
- capital finance
- consumer and industrial.

As a professional within GE you'll understand what you do, who your customers are and what they expect. Everything you do will be focused around growing the core business you represent. If you're in the energy business then you'll be focusing on a wide range of issues which may include:

- providing education and training in wind technology
- identifying and developing core skills to support the renaissance in nuclear energy
- developing distance learning materials and support mechanisms to support the planned UK introduction of smart meters.

What I'm saying here is that everything you do needs to show a direct line and impact to growing and supporting your core business. It doesn't matter what esoteric approaches you take (within reason) or the technology you use or which angle you take on social media; all that matters is that whatever you do helps to grow and support the core business. If you're not working on growing and supporting your core business then you're not aligned.

That said, some of you reading this may think that compliance training is not about growing a core business, but I would disagree. As we saw in an earlier chapter, approaching compliance training in the right way can be an excellent way to ensure your business thrives.

Keep your focus; question and challenge **everything** you do to ensure all your efforts are totally focused on growing and supporting your core business. If you're not helping to grow your core business then you're potentially putting in effort without result—rather like trying to make gold from lead, which as we saw earlier is a wholly unrewarding path to take.

As People Professionals, you should therefore do two key things:

- make sure you're absolutely clear on what your core business is, and
- do all you can to assist the growth and support of your core business

When you add value to business success
it's a great place to be!

Rule 3: Clear value propositions for the customer

I guess you've all heard of the "elevator pitch." Wikipedia describes this as:

> "A short summary used to quickly and simply define a product, service, or organization and its value proposition."

The purpose of the elevator pitch is to be able to succinctly describe, in a positive way, what value you add and underpinning a great elevator pitch is a value proposition which helps you paint a simple yet memorable story which describes this value.

Stop and think for a moment. If you were approached by one of your senior managers and asked "What do you do round here to help us make money?" what would you say? The chances are that you'd be rather flustered and blurt out something that isn't that positive!

I suspect that as a People Professional you won't tend to talk that often about value propositions or about creating value propositions as these things are often the reserve of the sales and development teams.

This might be a little unfair of me. However, having spent more than twenty-five years in this industry, the only time I've actually heard people talking about creating a value proposition was when I was running a commercial training company.

It's worth noting that value propositions are **not** just for commercial organisations, they are useful for **every** organisation, no matter what their business focus.

So what **is** a value proposition and how can it help with alignment?

Well, a value proposition is a promise of value to be delivered and a belief from the customer that value will be experienced. That may sound a little like "management speak" but stand back for a moment and take another look . . .

> "A promise that value will be delivered."

That means that you'll be making a promise that you know can be delivered. Not an empty promise, or a lie, but a promise you know you can deliver. That takes a lot of courage and planning and knowledge about what you do and what you can deliver. But it's only one side of the equation. The other side is:

> "A belief from the customer that value will be experienced."

The other side of the value proposition is that your promise will be believed. So not only must you have a great promise to make to your business or the customer, but it needs to be one that is believable.

At the heart of the proposition is the word "value." As professionals we use words like "value" all the time, but do we really know what we mean by value and, perhaps more importantly in this case, does our business believe us? Here's one take on what value actually is:

$$Value = Benefits - Costs$$

So the value of what we offer is the benefit we bring minus the cost of delivering that value. Most of our profession is plagued with the challenge of calculating and showing return on investment (ROI). In a later chapter I'll explore the whole issue of calculating benefit, but for now I'll continue to focus on creating the value proposition.

Although the concept of sitting down and actually working out a value proposition could well be an alien activity, as People Professionals you're competing on a daily basis for the limited resources your business has at its disposal and a well thought out value proposition demonstrates that you clearly understand the needs of your business and are responding accordingly.

Let's look at a value proposition in more detail.

Key components of a great value proposition

According to Neil Rackham, a best-selling author on the subject of sales and marketing, there are four main components of a value proposition. These are:

A. capability
B. impact
C. proof
D. cost

I'm using Neil's definition here because he's worked with sales teams from companies such as IBM and Xerox and he's consulted at the highest levels within McKinsey. I also like Neil's approach because it's simple and it directly applies to our profession. Let's look at each of the four components of a value proposition.

A. Capability

Way back in 1982, a landmark British TV series was broadcast called "Boys from the Blackstuff", which was a humorous but tragic look at the way a changing economy affected ordinary people.

One of the main characters in this series was Yosser Hughes, a large man desperate for work in order to keep his family together. Within this series, Yosser's catchphrase became "Gizza job" (give me a job) and "I can do that."

I mention this because although Yosser had a heart of gold and an inbuilt desire to provide for his family, he rarely had the capability for the work for which he was putting himself forward.

Within the People Profession, capability is the knowledge, skills and experience to deliver. You may not have all the capabilities in-house (and therefore may have to outsource or hire consultants) but without the ability to offer the capability you cannot begin to build a value proposition. Let's look at an example.

As a People Professional, you may already have certain capabilities within your business such as delivering classroom training, but you may want to branch out into other areas such as e-learning. Clearly, as a provider of classroom training, you'll already have capabilities such as:

- adult learning theory
- learning analysis and design
- designing great interactive learning
- understanding the needs of learners
- selling courses to learners (or their businesses).

So you may already have a number of the elements needed to demonstrate a capability in e-learning, but not all of them. It really doesn't matter how you add this capability into your mix; it could be by recruiting experienced resources or by partnering with an external e-learning provider. Either way you **must** be able to **demonstrate** capability otherwise you **cannot** build your value proposition.

B. Impact

It doesn't matter how much money you spend, or how many experts you involve, or how long it takes to deliver a solution; the fact is that you **must** deliver an impact. Impact can be measured in a host of ways, but essentially it's all about the positive change that you've made in your business or for your customers.

Impact could be:

- reduced costs
- increase in process speed
- fewer errors
- fewer accidents
- increased revenues
- reduced waste
- reduced time to competence for new entrants

The trick here is that just doing something (anything) is not enough. You **must** be able to measure impact, or show how you made an impact or show what impact you are likely to achieve, otherwise you'll be dead in the water. The best way to demonstrate impact is by some form of financial measure, although I realise that within the People industry it's never always that simple.

I've already mentioned that we'll be looking in detail at measurement and evaluation in a later chapter, but for now you need to know that some form of impact measurement is **essential** in developing your value proposition.

C. Proof

Another way of looking at proof is by answering the question:

So what?

I love that question; I always have done. It gets straight to the heart of so many issues yet it's so rarely used, perhaps because people are scared to use it.

I recently attended a meeting with a French senior executive. "You realise," he said, "that when someone asks you 'So what?' three times in a row you either know what you're talking about or you don't," and I totally agree!

As part of delivering a value proposition it's vitally important to be able to show **real** proof for what you're suggesting. Unfortunately in our profession demonstrating proof isn't always that easy. Let's see that in action by trying the following example:

For each of the following activities try and find some information, research papers, case studies etc. which demonstrate real proof of success. But don't just settle for statements such as "We think that XYZ made a difference"; try instead to find real hard evidence.

Here's the list—pick as many as you'd like to validate.

- e-learning is more effective than classroom training
- executive coaching increases the long-term performance of executives
- people fail to learn through classroom training or through formal lectures
- being a member of a professional institute is worth the yearly fee
- the correct use of psychometric tests means you hire better employees
- monetary reward systems (payment by results) do not always work
- multiple choice questions are the best type of question to use when you're assessing competency.

A really mixed bag, I think you'll agree, but take some time and see if you can find **real** proof of any of the above. I hasten to add these examples were chosen partly at random and some as a result of questions being asked across a number of industry forums.

Did you find any proof? Probably not that easy, was it?

As People Professionals we must **always** look for proof to substantiate the decisions we make. Relying on statements such as "I think . . ." or "It's a widely held belief that . . ." is a recipe for disaster. You need to show **real** evidence whenever possible.

But beware. I completely accept that ours is not a purely scientific industry (if at all!) It's rare for us to be able to write equations that really explain the interactions in our professional world. Newton, however, (clever old Isaac) could write an equation for calculating the gravitational force between any two objects in the universe.

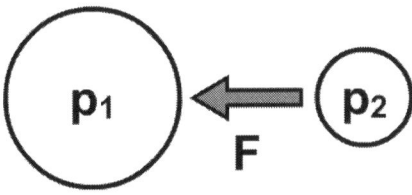

$$F = \frac{G*m_1*m_2}{r^2}$$

Where:

F is the force between the masses,
G is the gravitational constant = 6.6726×10^{-11}N-m^2/kg^2
m_1 is the first mass,
m_2 is the second mass, and
r is the distance between the centres of the masses

Take a look at the above equation, and no you're not going to have to calculate anything! Unlike science, the People Profession doesn't have the luxury of well-founded equations as ultimate proof. Despite all the psychometrics, aptitude tests, interviews and other assessment tools we cannot calculate (or predict) with certainty that a potential new hire will actually turn into a valuable employee and for that reason we need to work a whole lot harder to make our point or forever be labelled as the 'pink and fluffy' brigade. I realise that we do use pseudo-equations to try and describe the People world but these are more often than not approximations of a model, not real hard calculations deriving proof.

D. Cost

Let's return for a moment to our original equation:

$$Value = Benefit - Cost$$

We've already looked at the benefit costs of a value statement, so let's now turn our attention to the issue of costs, because when constructing your value proposition, the cost of your chosen approach is critical. Let's look at some extremes:

- the cost of a modern nuclear power plant is measured in terms of £billions
- the cost of extracting oil from the Gulf of Mexico or the Canadian Oil Sands is far higher than from 'traditional' drilling

In the above two cases, the cost of extracting that initial barrel of oil or producing that initial megawatt of electricity is overwhelmingly enormous, but this is outweighed by the benefits delivered over the lifetime of the project.

Although the people interventions that you deploy are unlikely to cost £billions, their cost will still have to be offset by the benefits. Here are a few examples:

- developing an e-learning course for a very small group of people that's only going to be used once may not ultimately be cost-effective
- using head hunters to recruit general staff is likely to be slow as well as incredibly expensive
- developing any people intervention (training, employee self-service etc.) when you have little or no capability may cost far more (certainly in terms of man-hours' effort) than buying a solution direct.

You therefore need to be able to calculate **accurately** and predict the cost of various interventions in order to build up an accurate value proposition. Remember that some companies will not reveal exactly how much they invested in a programme because of commercial confidentiality issues. However, as long as you can show some financial saving or reduction then this is fine.

And remember, costs can differ wildly and the cheapest approach isn't always the case in the long run.

Putting your value proposition together

We've looked at each of the components that make up a great value proposition, but what does one look like in real life? I searched high and low to find some examples because it's not all that easy to find value propositions within the People world! Once again I visited the Learning and Performance Institute's PardoFox survey of the *UK Training Top 50*.

I looked at the websites from the largest provider of training in the UK (by revenue). I couldn't easily see a value proposition which, if there had been one, should have jumped off the page at me.

I looked at the second largest—nothing there.

I then took a peek at the third largest . . . nope.

Then the fourth—nothing there either.

And the fifth largest. Guess what? Yup, nothing!

I'll be the first to admit that it was a very cursory look at each of the websites, but a value proposition needs to be there and "in my face", and I didn't see one at all. I kept searching and then, as I was approaching the high-end of the top twenty companies, I saw the following:

> "A new independent study shows that SkillSoft e-learners are more adaptable and achieve business results faster than other e-learners."

Wow, that's almost a value proposition—almost. SkillSoft even back up their claim with a link to an independent study white paper. Although I'd readily argue that some of the claims made within the white paper are a little tenuous, at least they've made a stab at delivering a sort of value proposition rather than merely (as is the case with virtually all the other top companies) just stating that "We do good training", or even "We want to change the world in which we live."

I also searched elsewhere for examples of a decent value proposition and have used the following example from Steria, the business process outsourcing company.

> "NHS Shared Business Services (NHS SBS) is Steria's 50:50 joint venture with the UK Department of Health. Using a shared service business model, NHS SBS is achieving huge economies of scale and is set to deliver £224 million savings over a ten year period."

Now that **is** a value proposition! Let's look at each of the four value proposition components in action:

Capability: Steria has enormous expertise in the area of joint ventures

Impact: 'Huge economies of scale'

Proof: 'Set to deliver £224 million savings'

Cost: Although the actual cost isn't mentioned, the savings were!

Value propositions can sometimes be internal documents which act as a blueprint or benchmark to ensure that all communications are consistent and aligned.

Value propositions are therefore used to:

- sell products and services to customers by explaining the benefits
- persuade partners to participate in joint ventures, or form strategic partnerships—both useful when you're trying to rapidly build capability!
- ensure internal departments such as HR, Finance and IT buy-in to new ideas
- ensure employees understand fully what you stand for as a company and what your values and aims are all about
- ensure suppliers appreciate the future impacts and pressures they may face.

A great example of this was when Steve Jobs was designing the iPhone and decided that he wanted scratchproof glass, rather than plastic. Jobs put his value proposition to Corning's CEO, and a previously non-mainstream product was brought to the fore. Corning's Gorilla Glass is now on every iPhone and iPad, not to mention a whole host of rival products. It's now **the** de facto material for screens for a whole range of devices.

Summary

People Professionals are increasingly battling to secure funds and resources for our initiatives. Resources will **always** be tight within business, but the development of a value proposition is an excellent way for the People Professional to put forward their case in a structured and logical manner; one which will appeal to senior executives and demonstrate that you have the needs of the business at heart.

Rule 4: Fine tune for the marketplace

Take a moment to sit back and relax . . .

Feeling OK?

Good . . .

Now think about the last time you really took one of your interventions or processes and fine-tuned it for the marketplace.

Let's be really honest. Do you constantly fine-tune your offerings for the marketplace, or do you just develop an intervention or process, then leave it alone, saying "That'll do"? I suspect it's probably the latter!

For the People Professional, fine-tuning can include:

- constantly updating learning and development interventions with relevant and up-to-date case studies,
- taking advantage of new technologies e.g. social media or the use of the internet for initial applicant screening, or for reaching targeted candidates,
- adapting your way of working to take advantage of newer communications methodologies e.g. Skype, virtual classrooms and virtual meetings, and
- staying abreast of the latest trends and developments, not only from standard People publications but also from sources such as *Harvard Business Review, The Economist, Wired* and so on.

Over the years I found that the People Profession is relatively quick to accept and implement new technologies, approaches and practices, although sometimes I wonder how many of these are truly introduced for the right reasons rather than a 'following the herd' or chasing the latest fad mentality.

This may seem a harsh statement. However, over the years I've seen almost every strange concept touted at conferences and exhibitions. I've seen drumming workshops, outward bound courses, massage therapies, more psychometric tools than I care to mention and the list goes on and on for far too long! I've overheard people at exhibitions working through a wish-list of what they need to look out for, rarely based on the needs of their business, but rather on the prevailing 'fashion' at the time! I've even come across what I can only describe as 'professional snobbery' whereby some organisations will talk down their noses at you if you're not using the latest software package, leadership technique and so on.

Fine-tuning for the market is, however, about much more than fashion; it's about understanding your business and how the environment in which it operates is changing—and spotting opportunities you can exploit to benefit your business. One example is the way in which the recruitment market has been transformed by the use of online technology.

Rule 5: Clearly communicate your strategy within the organisation and among other external stakeholders

I find it amazing how many businesses I've talked to about strategy over the years. The conversations are all pretty similar and they go something like this:

Me: So have you developed a strategy? (smiling and hoping for the right answer)

Business: (smiling) Oh yes, we've developed a strategy; a really good one!

Me: Brilliant, can I see it please? (wondering if this **will** actually be a strategy)

Business: I guess so. It's on this shelf somewhere . . . give me a moment and let me have a look. (embarrassed moments as the strategy is searched for)

Me: But if it's on the shelf then who knows about it? (already knowing what the answer is!)

Business: Knows about it? Well I (senior manager) know about it, isn't that enough? (sheepish looks all round)

Me: But what about others in the business, do they know about it? (oh, I so know the answer to this one!)

Business: Crikey no! You need to realise that not everyone has the capacity to understand a strategy, y'know!

Me: So . . . if others don't know about the strategy, how will they know what's important and what the priorities are and what they should be working towards?

Business: Well, eh, I guess . . . well er . . . (tumbleweed passes by)

OK, so I've embellished the story to make a point but the truth is that:

A winning strategy is of little use if nobody knows anything about it!

Sharing your strategy, both internally and externally, is an excellent way of signalling your intentions and gaining buy-in for what you're about to embark upon. Sharing your strategy demonstrates that you not only 'get' the key issues and challenges facing your organisation but that you also have appropriate solutions and mitigations in place. A good strategy says to your business "we understand the issues and are well-placed to deal with them".

Some of you might be horrified that a strategy could possibly be shared externally, but there are few large companies (and even small ones) that can't achieve their strategy all on their own. In order to be successful they **have** to share their strategy (or at least part of it) to remain successful. Here are a few examples:

- Airlines need to signal their intentions well in advance to ensure that aeroplane manufacturers and engine builders understand and can respond to their needs. After all, an aeroplane is hardly an off-the-shelf item! Perhaps the airlines want long haul, perhaps short haul. They almost certainly want cost-effective and fuel-efficient engines. None of this can be achieved without sharing a strategy.
- Major energy companies need to share their strategy in order to stimulate the supply chain. Nuclear power stations and large-scale wind farms need a massive investment in infrastructure and this cannot happen overnight. Indeed, it takes many years for supply chains to reach fully the levels required. Imagine just turning up on the doorstep of an organisation and trying to order 200 wind turbines; it's just not going to happen!

Naturally, there are certain market-specific and product-specific elements of your strategy that you'll keep hidden. Apple is certainly uber-secret when it comes to new products or release dates, but it could not bring new products to market without sharing its strategy with the various suppliers and manufacturers necessary to bring its products to life.

As for how you should best communicate your strategy, well I certainly don't intend to go through the process of explaining exactly how you can do this—there are literally dozens of books on the market to help you do that. What I would say though (and I'll look at this a great deal more in a later chapter) is that you absolutely must get your message out, simply and clearly, to all your stakeholders. For the People Professional that could mean:

- senior executives
- managers
- team leaders
- employees—both full-time and part-time
- contract staff and key business partners
- unions
- external suppliers

Remember that communication is not a one-off activity. You'll need to communicate continuously with your stakeholders in order to keep them informed about changes, progress and results and, of course, be prepared to answer honestly the questions that they may raise.

Let me give you an example . . .

I once worked with a large UK public organisation which wanted to introduce e-learning across its business. It already had a team of exceptionally competent trainers and designers whose only concern was that they might lose their jobs to the march of technology. Explaining the overall strategy to them was critical to gaining their support and commitment. When they realised that rather than jobs being lost, their role was going to get a whole lot more interesting, they actually became the champions for the strategy. Without adequate communication and honesty, the training team would have almost certainly fought the change to the detriment of all concerned.

Conclusions

Strategy is an often-used but ill-understood word. In this chapter you've learned about the five strategy rules which go together to make a great strategy. You've also learned about value propositions and the need to fine-tune your strategy as well as ensuring that you communicate your strategy in an honest and open manner to all of your key stakeholders

Remember that a strategy is your response to business issues—it is **not** solely dedicated towards showing how clever you are or how to plan to solve world hunger—and **always** start from the outside in!

Chapter 6: Activities

Here's a good time to reflect on your current strategy—assuming of course that you've got one!

Look at your current strategy (and if you haven't got one then now's a good time to start developing one) and check to see if your strategy:

1. starts from the outside in
2. supports the business and helps to grow the core business
3. contains key elements of a value proposition
4. is fine-tuned for the market place, and
5. is understood by everyone who needs to know.

7

Structure

"Every company has two organisational structures: The formal one is written on the charts; the other is the everyday relationship of the men and women in the organisation."

Harold S. Geneen
Businessman and former president of the ITT Corporation

Introduction

I recall a great story which happened when I was working with a team of senior managers in the energy sector. We were developing a new approach for a large multi £billion business, one that would begin to empower every employee and as a result release a massive amount of goodwill and energy to really deliver a step-change in business performance.

One of the senior managers (and I do mean senior) was mulling over the concept that you'd best understand as loose-tight management. He turned to the small team of us in a conference room and said:

> "I see it like this: if I'm a football manager then I know the rules of the game, I know what I can and can't do and I know where the boundaries are. But as manager it's my decision to organise the team the way I see fit, to play them in the best formation and structure for the game ahead."

This is the focus of this chapter—playing your team in the best way possible in order to be aligned with and deliver value to your business.

In this chapter we'll be looking at:

- the history of organisations and their structures, and
- the best way to play your own structure to ensure success.

The history of organisations and their structures

Have you ever wondered why an organisation is structured the way it is and why so many organisations have a "traditional" structure as shown below?

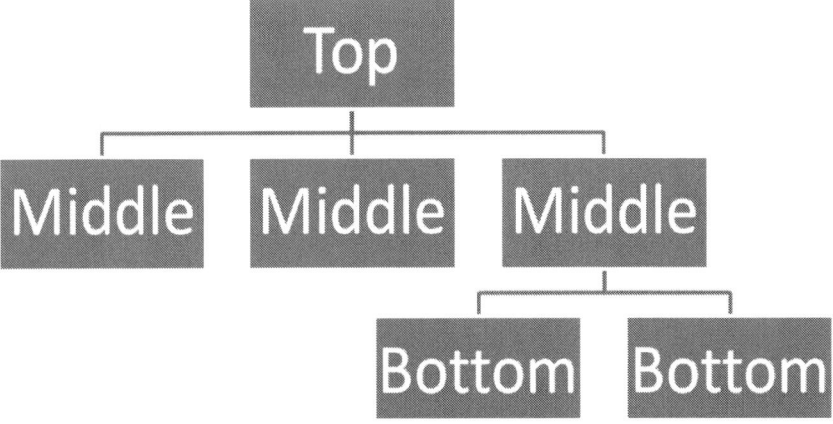

Maybe you've not wondered why the above structure is used by so many organisations, but here's a little history for you anyway . . .

The traditional hierarchical structure we know and love today was developed in order to control a large number of people in the simplest way possible. The two organisations which decided this was the best way to organise large numbers of people were:

- the military, and
- the church

The history of organisational structures dates back over two thousand years to when Roman general and statesman Cais Marius reformed the Roman legions into separate cohorts. His improvements to the structure and organisation of the Roman legion were profound and effective. Following

Cais's changes, legions had clear leaders, reporting lines and manageable chains of command—something that companies still use to this day.

The Catholic Church also adopted a similar hierarchical structure to ensure adequate control between the Pope and the priests.

Apart from the Roman legions (and later all armed forces) and the Catholic Church, there wasn't a need for anyone else to adopt these structures, simply because they weren't required anywhere else. Well, they weren't until the industrial revolution.

Officially taking place between 1750 and 1850, the industrial revolution was a period where massive changes in agriculture, manufacturing, mining, transportation and technology had a profound effect on the social, economic and cultural conditions of the time. Although it began in the United Kingdom, its modus operandi has spread throughout the world.

In essence, for the first time since the Legions and Church, the industrial revolution was a time when a large number of people needed to be organised and controlled in order to achieve a common end.

I find it interesting that over 260 years later—and despite all the advances we've had in business and business management—for the vast majority of organisations this 'original' structure is **still** in use today!

So for the past 2000+ years, whenever we've needed to organise a large number of people, this 'traditional' structure has been used; even the Cubs and Scouts are organised in the same way! But does it have to be like this?

According to Professor Gary Hamel in his Harvard Business Review article "First, Let's Fire All the Managers", he says:

> "How essential is it to have layers of executives supervising workers? Managers are expensive, increase the risk of bad judgment, slow decision making, and often disenfranchise employees. Yet most business activities require greater

coordination than markets can provide. Think of the countless hours that team leaders, department heads, and vice presidents devote to supervising the work of others. Most managers are hardworking; the problem doesn't lie with them. The inefficiency stems from a top-heavy management model that is both cumbersome and costly."

It's worth reading Gary's article to understand the real detail of what he's talking about, but I use this to point out two issues:

1. businesses **don't** all have to be organised in the same way, and
2. traditionally organised businesses are, by their nature, inefficient.

So what does this mean for you, and how does it affect alignment?

As People Professionals, I suspect that the structure of your business isn't always something that'll be at the forefront of your mind. I suspect that for many of you in large businesses who have inherited a department, the chances are that you're pretty much organised the way you were on day one of your tenure and that the shape of your business is almost certainly traditional in shape and operation.

Despite what you may think, research has shown that the core structure of any business isn't an indicator of success. There isn't a 'better' or 'best' way to organise people; it's what you do with them—how you play them—that makes the real difference.

I realise that the chances of your changing the shape of any part of your business may well be slim, but that doesn't matter; you don't need to change the shape of your business, just the way it operates. In order to become aligned, there are four attributes that your structure should deliver on, no matter what shape it is.

Organisations that have adopted the following four attributes can and do make a real difference in the workplace. The four attributes that I'll be expanding upon are:

1. flat and fast

2. simplify until it hurts
3. promote co-operation and the exchange of information, and
4. have the best people at the coal face.

Let's look at each one of these in turn . . .

Attribute 1: Flat and fast

I'd like to start by telling you a real story. A long, long time ago in a land far, far away called Norfolk there was a budding management trainee (me) embarking upon the first 'real' job of my career. I worked for a well-known high street retailer and we were in the process of refitting the Norwich store with a brand new 'look and feel', one we hoped would significantly increase revenue and profits for the business.

As part of this refit we had hired a small industrial unit on the outskirts of the city to hold all the new shop fittings and my task—together with one of the warehousemen—was to go and get rid of all the packing cardboard. A simple job you would think, but our clean cardboard, which was just the same as anything that would wrap your Amazon purchases today, was classed by the Council as industrial waste because it came from a business. That meant we couldn't put it in the cardboard bin at the local tip; oh no, that would be bad. Instead, we needed an industrial tipping licence (only available from County Hall) and this licence and the associated fee was connected to the size of your vehicle, not how much you were dumping.

Remember the World War Two movies, when air crews looked at silhouette boards of enemy fighters so they could identify them? Well, to this day, I still remember the man at County Hall showing me a silhouette board of trucks and lorries and saying, "OK then mate, which one is like yours?"

We needed a licence and had to know the size of our van and had to be told where to dump the cardboard. So many people, so much wasted time. And of course when we arrived at the industrial tip we were laughed at because they had no way of actually handling the pitifully small amount of cardboard we had!

But the story has stayed with me for two deep-seated reasons. Firstly, I got one hell of a shouting at for "taking so long to dump some bloody cardboard" and secondly, I have never forgotten how inefficient Norfolk County Council was at getting a simple task completed.

I'm sure that you also have your own stories of just how inefficient businesses can be and I'm glad you do, because this inefficiency could also be happening in your business—right now. That's what I want to get to the heart of here: the potential inefficiencies of your business and how you might go about addressing them.

Despite what many management books tell us, success isn't really impacted by the shape or structure of your business. It doesn't matter if you're a matrix business or a traditional hierarchical business, a for-profit or a not-for-profit business. One thing that really distinguishes any structure is that it's flat and fast. Let me explain.

Flat and fast structures are those that are stripped of bureaucracy wherever possible and with everyone empowered to act and make decisions at each stage of the process. Your structure should therefore be responsive to the needs of your business and the customers you serve. Can you **honestly** say that's the case with your business?

I'm now going to ask you to take a good hard look at your business and think about the following.

Try for a moment to think (honestly) about how long it takes to:

- approve a new learning intervention (you can define this any way you want to)
- hire an external consultant
- approve a member of your team attending an internal course or workshop
- approve a member of your team attending an external course or conference
- replace a member of your team who's left the business
- promote a member of your team
- give someone a pay rise, or

- respond to a member of your business who call/emails with a general enquiry.

I'm going to poke a little fun at a situation here in order to make a point. However, I wonder if the following spoof conversation make you wince or smile?

Business: We've got a problem and need your help to fix it.

You: Oh yes, we're the people to help you. What sort of problem do you have?

Business: Our contact centre isn't working as well as it should. We've got a new product launch coming up in a couple of weeks and our people need training.

You: Oh, they need training, do they? How do you know that?

Business: I've just bloody well told you! We've got a new product launch coming up and our contact centre isn't working properly. Our people are currently taking 20% longer to deal with customer calls than they should. Unless we can work out what's wrong and fix something fast then we're facing a car crash here!

You: But perhaps you're just experiencing a very high number of calls, or perhaps the calls you're getting are of a more technical nature, or perhaps your systems are just slow?

Business: Look, we've had a look at everything and we're sure it's a training issue. The systems are fine; the call volumes are as expected. We just need your help.

You: Mmmmm . . . . Have you done a TNA?

Business: What??!!

You: A Training Needs Analysis. Have you done one?

Business: What do I need to do one of those for?

You: Well according to the CIPD, one of the leading professional institutions in this field:

> "The identification of learning and talent development needs is based on the conduct of a formal or informal assessment of prevailing levels of skills, attitudes and knowledge, and any current or anticipated gaps, to inform decisions about the learning provisions required at individual, team or organisational level.
>
> The implementation of a formal learning needs analysis (LNA)—also sometimes known by alternative terms such as training needs analysis (TNA) or training and learning needs analysis (TLNA)—may be seen as a health check on the skills, talent and capabilities of the organisation (or part of the organisation). It is based on the systematic gathering of data about existing employees' capabilities and organisational demands for skills, alongside an analysis of the implications of new and changed roles for changes in capability."

Business: Are you bloody serious?

You: Oh yes, very. You see, until we carry out a thorough TNA it's impossible to fully ascertain the true nature of your requirements. You see, it could be that . . . . (droning on and on and on and on)

Business: Are you for real? I give up! AAARRRGGHH!

OK, I realise that I've rather embellished the story in order to make a point, but does the above seem a particularly flat and fast response? I would suggest not.

No matter how big your business, the more that people have to refer to others or go through a tortuous chain of command then the 'fatter' the business is. Be pragmatic, empower people and throw out bureaucratic approaches. Above all, as your acid test, look at everything from the point of view of people who have to do business with you. Look at everything you do and offer and see where you can make it better.

You can read all sorts of books and publications about how to empower people but do you know what people do who are really empowered—and I mean **really** empowered? Here's a story . . .

> Management guru Tom Peters tells a 1980s story about FedEx, the "absolutely, positively" overnight delivery company we all know. A telephone tower located atop a snow-covered mountain served the main FedEx call centre. The tower goes out of commission and the phone company can't get to the top of the mountain to repair it. A FedEx technician, on his own initiative, charters a helicopter to fly him to the mountaintop to fix the phone company's tower, assuring FedEx's call centre's ability to resume operations as soon as possible.

It didn't matter how FedEx was organised; the nub of this story is that things got done (and fixed) fast.

Attribute 2: Simplify until it hurts

The second attribute which will lead you to an aligned structure is all about making everything you do as simple as possible. It's often thought that the more complex something is then the 'better' it is. We all know, deep down, that that's so wrong, that simplicity has a beauty which is rarely found in business.

As Albert Einstein once said:

"You do not really understand something unless you can explain it to your grandmother."

I love this quote because all too often People Professionals are so wrapped up in what they do that if a parent or grandparent asks those immortal words "So what it is it you do?" they can only answer in crazy-mad-management-speak. It's sad but true; I've heard it too many times for it not to be true.

Over the years I've collected some real examples of "management speak" that will almost certainly make you smile:

From Norwich Union (now Aviva):

> "Where the policy is divided into a number of distinct arrangements ('Arrangements') where benefits are capable of being taken from an Arrangement or group of Arrangements separately from other Arrangements, then this policy amendment will not apply to any Arrangements in respect of which the relevant policy proceeds have already been applied to provide benefits. The policy amendment will apply to all other Arrangements under the policy."

From Capgemini Consulting:

> "Driving effectiveness, efficiency and global leverage through the Industrialization of our delivery capability, leveraging our global staff capability, people, tools and methods in a highly leveraged way."

From Manchester University:

> "This symposium aims to provide ethnographic and anthropological substance to the political philosophy of publicization. We hope to elucidate the ethnographic forms that the new public forums (Helga Nowotny et. al. call them agora) are taking in our anthropological contemporary. Society's political reinvention in an array of public objects is

modelled on, and casting off, new claimants and claims over the 'social contract': ethics, governance, trust, information, knowledge, are but some of the categories of association that are being re-deployed in the claim to make society more robust. Our aim in this symposium, then, is to investigate some of the forms that 'society' is taking today in its redistribution as public knowledge, illustrating with concrete examples the institutional and social journeys of knowledge in its promotion to 'public' status."

As with many of the examples in this book, I've gone to the extreme to make a point, but it is **essential** that you look to simplify everything you possibly can. Remember from the earlier chapter on strategy where I looked at the power and simplicity of value propositions? Well here's another reason to keep it simple.

To show just how everyday complex statements can be made into simple ones, here are some real examples from the Plain English Campaign who, according to their website, "oppose gobbledygook, jargon and legalese".

Before:

High-quality learning environments are a necessary precondition for facilitation and enhancement of the ongoing learning process.

After:

Children need good schools if they are to learn properly.

Before:

If there are any points on which you require explanation or further particulars we shall be glad to furnish such additional details as may be required by telephone.

After:

If you have any questions, please phone.

Before:

It is important that you shall read the notes, advice and information detailed opposite then complete the form overleaf (all sections) prior to its immediate return to the Council by way of the envelope provided.

After:

Please read the notes opposite before you fill in the form. Then send it back to us as soon as possible in the envelope provided.

Before:

Your enquiry about the use of the entrance area at the library for the purpose of displaying posters and leaflets about Welfare and Supplementary Benefit rights, gives rise to the question of the provenance and authoritativeness of the material to be displayed. Posters and leaflets issued by the Central Office of Information, the Department of Health and Social Security and other authoritative bodies are usually displayed in libraries, but items of a disputatious or polemic kind, whilst not necessarily excluded, are considered individually.

After:

Thank you for your letter asking for permission to put up posters in the library. Before we can give you an answer we will need to see a copy of the posters to make sure they won't offend anyone.

But don't just take it from me, or the Plain English Campaign for that matter. Jack Welch, former CEO of General Electric, was also passionate about simplicity. He said:

> "Insecure managers create complexity. Frightened, nervous managers use thick convoluted planning books and busy slides filled with everything they've known since childhood . . . . They worry that if they're simple, people will think they're simple minded. In reality, of course, it's just the reverse. Clear, tough minded people are the most simple."

Do you use thick convoluted words? Do you over-complicate messages and processes? Do you hide behind the management mumbo-jumbo because you just don't know how to make it simple? If you do then you've already seen that there's a real danger of becoming marginalised. I make no excuses for focusing so much on the use of simple language. As we've seen many times already within this book, the way in which People Professionals describe their work needs to be accurate, pithy and demonstrate value.

Sadly, as People Professionals, I feel that many of us continue to over-complicate what are really straightforward issues. Don't believe me? Read on!

According to Wikipedia (as an independent source), some of the characteristics of a Learning Management System (LMS) are:

- manager enrolment and approval
- boolean definitions for prerequisites or equivalencies
- integration with performance tracking and management
- planning tools to identify skill gaps
- curriculum, required and elective training requirements

Now step back for a moment and imagine you're speaking to a manager or client. What the hell are "boolean definitions for prerequisites or equivalencies" and who really cares?

Businesses are constantly talking about the simplicity of their processes, or how simple it is to use their website, or how simple it is to pay for goods and services etc. But do we really believe them? Be honest, how many systems or processes have you found that are **really** simple to use?

Apple has long been held up as a world leader in simplifying the complex. From the early day of the original Macintosh to the current day iPhones and iPods, Apple has always sought to make things simple.

According to Jonathan (Jony) Ive, Senior Vice President of Industrial Design at Apple:

> "Our goal is to try to bring a calm and simplicity to what are incredibly complex problems so that you're not aware really of the solution, you're not aware of how hard the problem was that was eventually solved."

Jony has also said:

> "Get rid of anything that isn't absolutely essential."

And I would totally echo Jony's sentiments; whenever you can, take time to weed out all the pointless steps in your processes, even down to looking at every box you ask someone to fill in or every link you want someone to click on your website.

Sticking with the Apple theme for a few moments more, Steve Jobs was also a man who totally believed in simplicity. As Jobs's biographer Walter Isaacson said about Steve:

> "He truly believed that simplicity was a virtue. Indeed, a statement often attributed to Leonardo Da Vinci adorned the early Mac manual: Simplicity is the ultimate sophistication."

Steve Jobs was renowned for making things as simple as possible. I know it's easy to look at the work of Apple and say "That's OK for Apple, but who else is doing this?" and expect a null answer, but so many companies have taken the potentially complex and made it a whole lot easier. For example:

- The design company Alessi who have made the Voile spaghetti measure and the Blip spoon rest and the Juicy Salif Citrus-squeezer but to name a few—just beautiful.
- Amazon and the one-click ordering process—simple idea, stunning results.
- Amazon (again) and the Kindle—just brilliant!
- The Apps store—sorry, another Apple example, but just so simple to use.
- Paying your car tax online—a UK government initiative that actually **works** and saves queues and hassle—brilliant!

I realise the above are all well-known examples of simplicity, but what about something a little more esoteric such as getting a blood test in Cheltenham?

"What?" I hear you ask. "A blood test? What's that got to do with simplicity?"

Take a step back for a moment and think about all the steps normally necessary to get a blood test done. For years I've been on the bone marrow donor list and a while back I received a letter saying that I was a possible match for someone who needed a bone marrow transplant. In the past I'd have had to take my special blood testing kit along to a hospital and plead to get a blood test done quickly rather than waiting for hours to be seen. Not in Cheltenham! There it's just like visiting a delicatessen:

1. you turn up at the hospital and go to the appropriate department,
2. you pick a number (just like you would at a delicatessen),
3. then you wait for your number to be called (everyone is dealt with in turn),
4. you get your blood taken by an exceptionally efficient and smiling nurse and
5. then you leave—job done!

That's it!

No fuss, no bother and a minimum of hassle. No booking in, no missed appointments and a service that deals with dozens of patients in a very short period of time.

Think like Amazon, think like Apple and think like Cheltenham Hospital and do all you can to make your products and processes just as simple as can be. People will thank you for it and people will remember.

Attribute 3: Co-operation and the exchange of information

Have you ever been to a meeting only to discover that you're the only one who doesn't know a critical piece of information about a key project or customer? I guess we've all been there at some point and thought to ourselves: "If only I'd known that then I wouldn't have done . . ."

Co-operation and the exchange of information within businesses is becoming more critical than ever before. The knowledge worker has certainly found their place within business and is set to stay for the foreseeable future.

For many businesses, the flow and access to knowledge can be the difference between success and failure. This is certainly true with pharmaceutical companies, which over recent years have dramatically altered the way they go about the business of drug discovery. No longer are huge labs with robotic-like machines churning out thousands of examples of potential medicines; instead there is now a massive flow of information and co-operation between drug companies big and small, between the traditional drug companies and the emerging bio-science start-ups. The realisation is that, far from keeping information secret and in silos, the power of information and knowledge can only be reached if it's shared.

The drug giant Novartis has even designed its latest campus in Boston Massachusetts in such a way as to stimulate information sharing and actually encourage serendipitous meetings—the sort from which some great new breakthrough may emerge.

As People Professionals we have much to learn from organisations such as Novartis; the sharing of knowledge and information enables everyone to make sense of the world around them. Flat and fast businesses will be hugely stimulated by creating rapid access to and exchange of information at all levels of the business. As People Professionals, stimulating this exchange is another critical step to creating alignment; the more the business shares information about what you do, or what value you can add, the more likely you are to be understood and to succeed.

Attribute 4: The best people up front

It's a sad fact, but as people become better, more experienced, wiser and of more use to a business, so they are removed further and further from the front line.

I've mentioned the benefit, indeed necessity, of empowering the people who are closest to your customers and ensuring they deliver best value.

Rather than hiding your good people at the back, consider putting them directly on the front line, directly in front of your business or customers. Make the good people accessible, allow their talent to be tapped into and make sure they're part of the collaboration and information sharing mentioned above.

Your best people are more likely to solve problems swiftly and efficiently, more likely to speak with authority and more likely to provide some kudos for your department. Shame they tend to all be hidden away for most of the time!

Conclusions

The structure of your business and department can bring real success. Traditional structures have been with us for thousands of years and are sometimes seen to be the cause of sluggishness and unwanted bureaucracy, but this is not the case. It's not the way that you organise your business, but the way you organise your people.

In this chapter we've learned that structures need to be flat and fast, that everything you do needs to be simplified as far as possible, that you need to promote co-operation and the free exchange of information and that you need to have your best people accessible to your business and to your customers.

Having a structure that can respond at speed and which offers simple, quality access to knowledge is one that is truly aligned. Fail to achieve this and you'll be looked upon as being slow, bureaucratic, awkward, obstructive and obsolete.

Chapter 7: Activities

Let's look at the structure of your business or department and see how it compares. Answer each of the following questions as honestly as possible:

Question	All of the time	Some of the time	Never
My business works in a fast and flat way, responding quickly to the needs of the customer.			
My department works in a fast and flat way, responding quickly to the needs of the business.			
My business continually works to simplify processes and to reduce waste.			
My department continually works to simplify processes and to reduce waste.			
My business is open and readily promotes co-operation and access to key information.			
My department is open and readily promotes co-operation and access to key information.			
My business puts the best people up front and empowers them to do an outstanding job.			
My department puts the best people up front and empowers them to do an outstanding job.			

Now look at the answers you gave.

- Is your business doing all it can to make the best of its structure and to serve its customers as best as possible?
- Is your department doing all it can to make the best of its structure and to serve the business as best as possible?

Depending on your answers above, what changes do you think need to be made? How would you go about making those changes?

8

Culture

"The thing I have learned at IBM is that culture is everything."

Louis V. Gerstner
Former CEO of IBM where he was largely credited with
reversing the company's declining fortunes

Introduction

People Professionals are forever talking about culture—the culture of the business, the culture of the customers' business, and the ideal culture for learning, for talent, for coaching and so on. We talk about "changing culture", about "improving culture" and about "creating culture", but do we **really** know what culture is all about and how it can be used to achieve alignment? Probably not!

Everywhere I look the culture never seems to be as good as it could be, or rather it always seems to be better somewhere else! Article after article describes how the culture within a business is critical to success, but in all these articles the one thing that seems to be overlooked is the culture of your professional department in the business itself!

In this chapter I'll be looking at creating an aligned culture, which means:

- establishing and sticking to clear business values
- inspiring everyone to do their best
- rewarding achievement, and
- providing a challenging and fun working environment.

Before we start it's worth noting that for the purposes of this book I'm defining culture as "the way we do things around here". I'm not going to get deep into the esoteric issues which sometimes underpin the culture of a business; it's just about how things are done. So, without further ado, let's get cracking.

Establishing and sticking to clear business values

Values. We hear about values all the time in business, almost as much as we hear about culture! Businesses talk about their values as though they are some form of traded option, as though the values of a business actually make a difference to success.

But do they? Do values **really** make a difference?

In his book, "Built to Last: Successful Habits of Visionary Companies" James (Jim) Collins alks at length about the values that the more successful companies (he calls them "visionary") have and hold dear to their business hearts.

It's interesting to note that for almost all of the visionary companies, making money is **not** at the top of their list of values. Johnson & Johnson (for example) have a credo which they have worked with for years. The first responsibility on the credo states that:

> "We believe our first responsibility is to the doctors, nurses and patients, to mothers and fathers and all others who use our products and services. In meeting their needs everything we do must be of high quality. We must constantly strive to reduce our costs in order to maintain reasonable prices. Customers' orders must be serviced promptly and accurately. Our suppliers and distributors must have an opportunity to make a fair profit."

The second responsibility of the credo focuses on employees, the third responsibility on communities and the fourth and last responsibility on stockholders.

Interesting, eh? Stockholders come last—bottom of the list. Customers come first. I wonder how that compares with the values adopted by other major businesses?

A swift tour of the internet courtesy of Google (as always) revealed some of the values of the following major businesses:

Google:	Focus on the user and all else will follow
Amazon:	Customer obsession
BP:	Safety
IBM:	Dedication to every client's success
BBC:	Trust is the foundation of the BBC: we are independent, impartial and honest
HSBC:	Dependable and do the right thing
Facebook:	Focus on impact
Dell:	Delivering results that make a positive difference
Microsoft:	Creating a great place to work
McDonalds:	We place the customer experience at the core of all we do
Marks and Spencer:	Delivering excellent standards consistently

ACTIVITY:

> For each of the above take a look at the values of each business and decide if you think their values match with "the way we do things round here." Mark each on a scale of 1 to 5 where 5 is a perfect match and 1 is miles away.

Here are some of my thoughts on a few of the above. You may or may not agree, but it'll get you thinking.

Amazon: I totally agree with their stated values—everything about the company is focused on making the customer experience better.

BP: Safety, a value—really? But if that's really the case then what about the Texas City and Deepwater Horizon disasters? Sadly, BP's past contains instances where safety was not judged to be as high on the agenda as it should have been. Remember—"it's the way we do things round here" and BP hasn't actually demonstrated that value in recent years.

HSBC: Dependable and do the right thing—sounds impressive, but would that be why (as I am writing this very chapter) HSBC is in talks to settle a major international money laundering claim?

Values, it seems, can therefore be a help or a hindrance to any business. I should point out that I Googled far more businesses than are listed above in search of their values. Unfortunately, from the Google results (and it's no fault of Google), it wasn't always that obvious what the values were of the businesses I was checking on. For the most part, businesses merely state a collection of corporate "buzz words" and wide-ranging "feel good" statements rather than sending out any clear messages as to what they **really** stand for.

Returning to Johnson & Johnson (the visionary business with the credo), their deeply held beliefs about their customers was clearly demonstrated during the time of the Tylenol crisis. Although you can easily find out about it online, the key elements of the story are that Tylenol was being tampered with and poisoned in stores. The result? Johnson & Johnson withdrew the product and developed tamperproof packaging before releasing the product back to the public.

The cost to Johnson & Johnson was millions of dollars; however, the actions were totally aligned with the values of the organisation. Lives were potentially saved, the Tylenol brand was certainly protected and there are many who feel that in the longer term, the Johnson & Johnson brand was strengthened as a result.

Compare this with the approach taken by Perrier, at the time the leading UK brand for bottled water and with values and a brand identity based around the concept of "natural purity". Finding unwanted benzene in their product certainly wasn't ideal and the company had to withdraw 160 million bottles worldwide. When the story broke Perrier, unlike Johnson & Johnson, didn't know what to do or how to respond properly and as a result the effect on the brand and organisation was substantial. If you want to see the **real** impact, try looking for substantial quantities of Perrier ware on the shelves of UK supermarkets today and you'll see what I mean.

So, you may ask, why these stories about two different organisations and how on earth can these apply to you as People Professionals?

The underlying learning from these stories is that Johnson & Johnson not only established strong values for their organisation, but stood by them in times of crisis; an approach that not only provided them with strong guidance, but saw them through these tough times.

Values without substance or follow-through are nothing more than empty promises.

As People Professionals do you have a set of values you believe and abide in, or do you merely have a set of guiding principles that will crumble at the slightest sign of pressure or trouble?

As People Professionals, it's important that you develop a core set of values that will support and guide your decisions during tough times.

Consider this—what's really at the heart of your business values? Is it:

- customers?
- your business?
- learners?
- leaders?

- results?
- something else—maybe profit, or advancement, or self-interest?

Once you know which factors lie at the heart of your values you can then develop appropriate words, meanings and actions to support them.

Remember . . .

Values without substance or follow-through are nothing more than empty promises.

Make sure that the values of your business or department are substantially more than just paying lip service to something fancy or some trend that sounds "OK". They **must** be real and **must** "live" when times are tough.

Inspire everyone to do their best

I think it's easy to forget but as People Professionals we have a major role to play as leaders in our businesses. People look to you for direction and a sense of how life is going and what's important and what they should focus on. But what really inspires everyone to do their very best? What do people look for in a leader that will actually make a **real** difference?

In an ongoing project surveying tens of thousands of working people around the world, James Kouzes and Barry Posner asked:

"What do you look for and admire in a leader?"

The survey highlighted honesty as the number one requirement for a leader. The second-highest—they should be forward-looking (72% of all respondents wanted this). Interestingly, as the seniority of respondents increased, so the emphasis on being forward-looking rose to 88%.

When compared to the question "What do you look for and admire in a colleague?", the difference was astounding. Only 27% of respondents felt forward-looking was of importance in colleagues—a full 50% less than in leaders.

Let's be totally honest. There are hundreds of studies that have been conducted into leadership qualities, all of which have shown slightly different traits regarding what makes a great leader.

Although the Kouzes and Posner study indicates "honesty and forward-looking" as key traits, other studies have indicated that the following may also be the 'key' to leadership success:

- honesty
- openness
- communication
- authenticity
- emotional intelligence
- confidence
- knowledge
- leading by example
- coping with change

The hard facts are that there are dozens of leadership traits, so picking just a handful and claiming they are the 'magic view' is a rather tall order.

What is clear though is that, as a leader, you cannot do it all by yourself. This isn't about delegation or effective time-management; this is about ensuring that by being open and honest, having values and holding true to them and ensuring that your people are clear about their purpose, you will create a culture that will inspire everyone to do their best. Releasing the energy and enthusiasm of your team is essential in creating and maintaining the correct culture.

Reward achievement

As Jack Welch (former CEO of GE) once said, "Reward achievement with pay and praise, but keep raising the bar." I mean, if there's one thing that People Professionals should know about its reward and recognition!

I dread to think how many books, articles and studies have been written about the effects of reward on performance and the various approaches to both the claimed business and personal rewards both in the short—and long-term.

I don't propose to give a sermon on this subject as, at its heart, it's all pretty simple. In order to reward achievement, there are four key issues you should address. As People Professionals you'll no doubt already have read copious amounts about this subject, but in essence the four key sub-issues are:

- reward achievement with praise
- reward achievement with money
- keep raising the performance bar
- create a sense of ownership and belonging

1. Reward achievement with praise

When Ken Blanchard wrote the original and blockbusting book "The One Minute Manager", one of the themes of the book was praise and recognition through the phrase "catch someone doing something right for a change".

Praise achievement by all means but make sure that it's achievement and not just doing a job. Don't over-praise someone just for the sake of it. Catching someone doing their job isn't merely enough; you need to catch them making a real difference, a real impact within the business.

2. Reward achievement with money

As I'm writing this book I'm very conscious that we're still fighting the after-effects of a global banking crisis which, according to many commentators, was fuelled and driven by greedy bankers chasing larger and larger bonuses. As time goes on we're discovering more and more that greed and the pursuit of personal gain were key personal drivers of this crisis.

But is this really surprising? According to a study by Cornell University, giving a one percent raise boosts employee job performance by roughly two percent but offering the same amount of money in the form of a bonus can improve job performance by almost twenty percent—a strong indication (if ever it were needed) that bonuses can and **do** drive performance.

I appreciate that it may not be in your gift to devise a monetary reward scheme at your business. However, you should do all you can to ensure that your team is financially rewarded as best as possible for making the **right** contributions.

When he was at GE, Jack Welch developed a reward mechanism where senior executives running the various businesses had to outperform the market in order to receive a bonus. His view was that in a rapidly rising market it's easy to do well, but not easy to do better.

As People Professionals you should certainly consider the most appropriate way to reward your team. Money clearly isn't everything . . . .

3. **Keep raising the bar**

As People Professionals, we always want our employees and ourselves to do the very best possible at all times. In the world that is Kaizen and Six Sigma and Continuous Improvement, there is a constant necessity to keep raising the performance bar.

What's OK this year is mediocre next year. What's great this year is barely acceptable in two or three years' time. And it's not just the onset and emergence of the internet that is causing this. Take Formula One, for example; the relentless push for more speed year after year after year.

I've been privileged to to visit McLaren, one of the most successful Formula One businesses of all time and an organisation with a seemingly unquenched passion for constantly raising the performance bar.

Ron Dennis, the key driver (no pun intended) behind the business, pushes performance on a daily basis. His search for perfection is legendary.

When building the McLaren Technology Centre in Woking, Surrey (a world-renowned facility designed by Norman Foster) he was amazed that the soap dispensers in the toilets could, on occasion, drip soap onto the floor. For most people, the simple solution would be to fit a drip tray, but not so for Ron, who redesigned the soap dispensers so they just wouldn't drip at all. Raising the bar—always.

As People Professionals, do you raise the bar all the time? Do you push your team to raise the bar, or do you merely accept that 'OK' or 'close enough' will do for now? Challenge yourself on a daily basis to make next week's performance even better than today's and keep repeating this!

4. Create a sense of ownership and belonging

Are your team members turning up day after day and 'just' doing a job, or do they actually feel they 'own' part of the business and 'belong' in what they do? Can you give this sense of belonging, or are you just making sure that people 'follow the rules'?

In a (now famous) book "Maverick!" by Ricaro Semler, Ricardo talks about how he took a once 'normal' business and by applying common sense and giving people a real sense of ownership, he transformed this Brazilian business. The transformation though wasn't just 'pink and fluffy' stuff; Ricardo increased turnover from US$4 million in 1982 to US$212 million in 2003. That's real results!

But Brazil is a long way from a London-based IT training company. Founded by Henry Stewart (whose idol happens to be Ricardo Semler), Happy Computer set out to be a totally different IT training company, and it's succeeded. Henry has built a very successful business around trusting people and giving them a sense of ownership. Though far too many to list here, the awards and plaudits from individuals and industry alike are almost overwhelming. Henry has shown what can **really** be achieved if you believe in people.

You can read the books by Ricardo and Henry (Relax: A Happy Business Story) and learn about what they did and the results they achieved. It's nothing expensive or difficult, but it **is** radical when compared with the corporate drudgery that exists for most of us. One thing they have both achieved—without question—is a team of people totally aligned with the business; now that **is** a result!

5. Provide a work environment that is fun and challenging

Take a moment to look at the following list and consider whether these businesses either provide a great working environment, one that is fun, one that is challenging, or one that is all three. Here's the list:

- Happy Computer
- Semco
- Google
- Apple
- WM Gore and Associates
- 3M
- Ben and Jerry's

Make sure that as well as looking at the 'fun and challenging' elements of the above businesses, you also look at the results they've achieved year after year . . . you may be surprised!

Conclusions

Culture, or "the way we do things round here", is one of the key building blocks for achieving alignment and success. Culture can make or break a business and should, at the very least, be tightly aligned to the values of the business. A mismatch of culture and values will prohibit alignment and can also be the source of a number of long-term business problems.

As People Professionals, it's your role to identify and promote the culture most aligned to the values of your business and to do all you can to ensure that "the way we do things round here" is always focused on achieving the right thing at the right time.

Chapter 8: Activities

Here's a great time to reflect on your current culture. Take some time to review this chapter and then make a note of the top five things you think you need to improve on and list them below.

1.

2.

3.

4.

5.

9

Execution

"Strategy gets you on the playing field, but execution pays the bills."

Gordon Eubanks
Microcomputer industry pioneer who worked in the early
days of Digital Research

Introduction

I adore the quote at the head of this chapter. When writing a book it's never easy to find quotes that are direct, pithy and new. But Gordon's quote has it all.

As we've seen so far in this book, taking time and effort to develop an excellent strategy is clearly a key starting point and in developing a strategy you'll also have developed a value proposition which is so critical in gaining recognition for the work you're doing. But as I've already said, having a great strategy is of little use if you do nothing with it!

In general, People Professionals are relatively quick to adopt and implement new technologies and practices, although sometimes I wonder how many of these are truly introduced for the right reasons rather than being some kind of knee-jerk 'cat chasing the dot on the wall' reaction in order to please senior management.

I'll admit that I'm speaking from the heart here, but over the years (as I've already mentioned) I've seen so many fads tried and then put to one side that I often wonder how much real 'doing' People Professionals manage to achieve in a given period of time.

Here's a little teaser for you. Five frogs are sitting on a log. Four decide to jump off. How many are left? Answer: five. Why? Because there's a massive difference between deciding to do something and actually doing it!

In this chapter we are looking at the issues of execution and making sure that as People Professionals we actually deliver on a strategy and promises. Before we go any further let's be really clear about one thing . . .

<h2 style="text-align:center">A failure to deliver is a failure.</h2>

There are three key issues that People Professionals need to focus on to ensure they execute flawlessly. These are:

1. always deliver to meet expectations,
2. make sure the front line is really empowered, and
3. work tirelessly to improve productivity and eliminate excess waste.

1. Always deliver to meet expectations

According to Matt Haig's book "Brand Failures":

> "Henry Ford mastered mass production; McDonald's has mastered mass service production. It has done so through strict adherence to simple beliefs. Quality, cleanliness and uniformity are the basis of the McDonald's brand."

I'm not here to overly promote McDonald's. However, the example mentioned is mentioned for a very good reason; McDonald's continually ensures that delivery meets expectations. When you go into a McDonald's or use the drive-through, you know exactly what you're going to get. The organisation works exceptionally hard in ensuring that delivery meets the customer's expectation, time after time after time.

As People Professionals, there are a number of things that you'll need to deliver time and time again. These may include:

- developing courses or interventions
- delivering training courses
- coaching and mentoring
- recruiting new members of your team

Can you honestly say, hand on heart, that as a People Professional you always deliver products and services that meet expectations? Probably not! Delivering products and services that continually meet expectations is a never-ending task. According to the well-respected PZB Servqual model:

Quality = Perception - Expectation

Put simply, the quality that someone feels they get from a service is their perception of what they received minus their expectations. If their perception of the service is less than their expectations then the quality will be seen to be lower. Achieving the position of meeting the expectations of your business or customer is not easy; be very aware of that. Businesses have strived for years to achieve the almost magical position of being seen as a quality business, i.e. delivering what's expected. Think for a moment what would happen to Apple if they were to deliver a shoddy product, or to John Lewis if they were suddenly to abandon their focus on customer service.

People Professionals may sometimes feel that they're in the product market; perhaps they're selling pre-developed courses, authoring systems, other software solutions, or preconfigured psychometric tests. In truth though, we are **all** in the service industry and we mustn't forget that, because in the service industry achieving consistent execution day after day after day is exceptionally difficult. We know and appreciate that the people landscape is changing at a constant and at times alarming rate. What was once leading edge is now the norm and as People Professionals you need to be able to alter your delivery to meet ongoing adjustments in expectations. A few years ago we would wait for decent service or for the right product—but not today. Today the world revolves around speed and convenience (as mentioned in earlier chapters) and it's about having it **now**.

People Professionals need to be acutely aware of changes in business and operations and alter and enhance their offerings to meet the needs of an ever-changing market. So focus on ensuring that your delivery is spot-on and keep looking out for trends that you'll need to adopt to maintain a high level of quality.

2. Make sure the front line is really empowered

I always like to think of the front line as being 'any place where you interface with the customer'. This could include:

- a trainer delivering courses to an internal or external audience
- coaching or mentoring colleagues or clients
- recruiting a new member of your team or a customer's team
- providing employment advice
- giving a presentation and so on.

Businesses have long recognised that the point at which a customer interacts with the business is critical to success and that empowering people to deal with situations is a sure-fire way to support flawless execution. I'm sure you've been in a situation where you're faced with someone who, knowing that the information they're holding in their hands is wrong, looks at you and says, "Sorry, there's nothing I can do about this." Empowerment? Hardly! Compare this with two other companies that are world famous for their empowerment and execution—Nordstrom and Amazon.

Nordstrom is a US retailer famous for its employee handbook. For many years employees were given a single 5" x 8" grey card containing just seventy-five words. It's such a landmark that it's worth reproducing here.

"Welcome to Nordstrom

We're glad to have you with our company. Our number one goal is to provide outstanding customer service. Set both your personal and professional goals high. We have great confidence in your ability to achieve them.

Nordstrom Rules:

Rule #1: Use best judgment in all situations. There will be no additional rules.

Please feel free to ask your department manager, store manager, or division general manager any question at any time."

OK, things have changed and Nordstrom now provides a whole booklet of additional information, much of it legal, but I'm sure you get the picture. The experience at Nordstrom is legendary because the business is incredibly passionate about ensuring that employees are empowered to deal with any issues in the manner they see fit. It's a really tough thing to do, to let an employee make decisions, but it's absolutely essential to achieving flawless execution. Each time a decision has to be passed up the management chain it causes delays, costs money and wastes resources.

And now to Amazon, which states that it wants to be "the best customer service company in the world". As Amazon CEO, Jeff Bezos says:

"If there's one reason we have done better than any of our peers in the Internet space over the last six years, it is because we have focused like a laser on customer experience, and that really does matter, I think, in any business. It certainly matters online, where word of mouth is so very, very powerful."

Amazon's customer service has been built up over the years and despite being a relatively new company (it only went live in 1995) there are thousands of stories circulating about them—all positive. Their introduction of the *Kindle* has only increased that status as people around the globe echo the great service they receive. Let me add one other.

In writing this book I took the rather old-fashioned approach of writing everything by hand in a large A4 Moleskine folio—expensive perhaps—but it's one of the few journals that doesn't fall apart, will take ink without bleeding through the pages and can also survive some pretty rough treatment. I urgently needed some new Moleskine folios and some other supplies and turned, as always, to Amazon. I asked for the delivery to be sent to my mother's house as I was staying there for a few days. For the first time ever, the package didn't arrive. I checked the delivery tracking information and I could see that the carrier was clearly stating that it had delivered my goods two days ago. I decided to contact Amazon to see what was going on, and here's where the magic began.

Firstly, there was an option for them to call me. They did this immediately—wow!

The person who called me was sympathetic and checked with the delivery company right then and there. Because they couldn't get a satisfactory answer they said they had already shipped my order again, for free, and that they would sort out the original order with the courier.

As a customer I was dealt with courteously, my issue was resolved without my having to repeat myself a number of times over and Amazon made sure that I had my journals the very next working day. The person on the phone was totally empowered to solve my issue and this they did with consummate expertise—and boy did it show! Amazon executed flawlessly.

The challenge this story raises—and which I place on you—is that as People Professionals can you honestly say that your front line staff are really empowered to deal with issues in the way they are at Nordstrom and Amazon?

I mean **really** empowered?

Or are they just rule-followers who constantly have to refer issues to middle managers when something goes wrong?

Empowering your front line will result in a number of major benefits. Things will get done faster, people will feel more involved with the business and customers, either internal or external, will receive a much higher level of service. Empowered people deliver aligned organisations; you've just got to want to work hard enough to make it a reality.

3. Work tirelessly to improve productivity and reduce excess waste

When, honestly, did you last take a really hard look at the processes within your business and see if there's any opportunity of eliminating waste or making the process better? The chances are that you, your processes and your way of operating have changed little since you first put them into effect. Perhaps it's time to spring clean your processes and operations using techniques that enable lean operation.

The concept of lean is nothing new. It was started by Toyota after the Second World War and to this day Toyota is still seen as being the pathfinder for these techniques. Lean is all about doing more and more with less and less, by eliminating waste. "Muda" is Japanese for waste, so Toyota's focus is about reducing muda in as many places as possible. "But surely," you'll cry out, "as People Professionals we do not waste resources. After all, we're not making steel or power stations; we're just helping people be better at their jobs!"

Well, let's stand right back and have a really good hard look at where we'll generate waste (muda) on a daily basis:

- sending too many emails or emails that are information—rather than action-based,
- sending emails that are just too long or contain far too many attachments,
- failing to pre-screen candidates via telephone interviews,
- ordering too many dinners or coffees for workshop delegates,
- making people travel unnecessarily to meetings and workshops,
- failing to make the best use of virtual meetings and web-based communication technologies,
- wasting hours in meetings by not sticking to the agenda or having no agenda at all,
- sending out materials to staff that are just going to end up in the bin, and
- not using both sides of a piece of paper.

The list naturally goes on and on and on . . .

As People Professionals, we're one of the few groups of people who get the wonderful opportunity to interface on an ongoing basis with virtually everyone in our business. Not too many other professions can claim this and this ongoing interface is a fantastic opportunity for reducing waste and generating value. There's a great opportunity for you all to embark on embedding lean processes and not only save money but also time. Saving time and money is a sure-fire way to demonstrate your alignment!

Here are some facts regarding the environmental impact of electronic communications and processes:

- the carbon footprint of an email is 4g of CO_2
- the carbon footprint of a long email with an attachment is 50g of CO_2
- an email has the carbon footprint of about one sixtieth of a letter. Great unless you mail shot sixty times more emails than you ever used to do with letters!
- according to Gartner, data centres already account for 25% of carbon emitted and all energy consumed by the ICT sector
- Google's Oregon data centre, when full, will consume about the same amount of power as the city of Newcastle, UK, and
- even a mortgage (£100,000 @ 5%) generates 800g of CO_2 per year

One of my clients discovered that the largest increase in electricity use at their head office resulted from the additional requirement for more servers caused by people storing more data. This is known as the rebound effect, i.e. when something becomes easier or cheaper then we tend to do more of it. Because people didn't clean out their electronic storage my client was facing a potentially uncontrolled rise in electricity use. It's not always easy to deal with these issues, but the positive results are clearly measurable for the business.

Returning to the earlier facts, businesses can't just stop sending emails or storing data but it's definitely possible to turn waste into value. Perhaps your business doesn't actually need a printed booklet of all the courses it offers employees. Perhaps instead employees can be booked electronically onto courses and manage these bookings themselves, as is now becoming more widespread in large companies as self-service people products are increasingly rolled out. Even the simplest change could save you thousands of pounds per year. Here's an example.

Two of the professional institutes to which I belong (no names mentioned) issue membership certificates. One institute issues your certificate at the time you're accepted as an associate, member or fellow and only updates the certificate should your membership be upgraded. The other institute issues a certificate **every year**. That's thousands of pieces of paper, all colour-printed, posted out to tens of thousands of members in specially stiffened envelopes, **EVERY YEAR!** Add to that the cost of postage, labels and the physical manpower required to make this happen and the waste is sizeable. If ever there was a great chance to save money, reduce waste and reduce manpower then here it is!

These small steps can make a real difference to your business and will be **really** noticed by the senior managers. People Professionals are almost legendary for wanting to increase their budget each year, or pushing back and moaning when budget cuts loom. Actively reducing waste is a great way of showing that you're aligned to the business and 'doing your bit'.

Here's a question for you: How long does it take to make a can of Coca-Cola? When thinking about the answer you'll need to include everything needed to make the product, from mining the aluminium, to making the can, to actually getting the product into the supermarket. Here are four options for you to choose from. I'll give you the answer a little later. The total time taken to make a can of Coca-Cola is:

- 19 days
- 119 days
- 219 days
- 319 days

Now while you're thinking about that, turn your mind to your own profession. How long do you think it takes to develop a piece of e-learning or to design and implement a management development programme?

Again, that's everything from initial request to final delivery. I'll give you a few choices but does it take:

- hours?
- days?
- weeks?
- months?

OK, I realise that the answer depends on hundreds of variables, but let's take a moment and walk through what might be a typical route for developing a new e-learning course. I appreciate that only some of you reading this book will actually develop e-learning, but the basic approach will suffice for whatever requests are placed upon you. So here's a typical route:

1. receive the request,
2. conduct a training needs analysis,
3. demonstrate that the request is actually a business requirement,
4. decide on the overall approach and development,
5. gain approval,
6. gain budget approval,
7. decide whether to develop the e-learning internally or externally,
8. if using an external organisation then develop an invitation to tender (ITT),
9. send ITT to external companies,
10. review submissions,
11. make your choice of development partner etc., etc., etc.

You could end up with dozens of separate steps which may also include deciding upon technology platforms, assessment criteria, integration with internal systems and so on. Just take a few moments and look at the list above. As a People Professional, what do you think you could do to reduce waste and make processes such as this faster and better?

I once ran a commercial training company and each quarter we developed the forward schedule for our public classroom courses. I dread to think how many man-hours we wasted on this task and how many mistakes we made in trying to second-guess competitor prices, the number of courses we may actually sell, the key locations that we'd need, potential demand and so on! And yet we knew that this was a critically important task and we knew we'd definitely have to do it four times a year, every year, and despite this we **never** invested time in making the process better either for ourselves or our customers. This was a great opportunity missed.

Now back to the earlier question of how many days it takes to make a can of Coca-Cola. Did you guess correctly at 319 days? That's right, from mining the aluminium ore to putting the can on a supermarket shelf takes 319 days for a can of Coke. That's almost a year!

Reducing waste from any of the stages to get a can of Coca-Cola to the customer will have a major impact. Perhaps there are processes within your business that can be trimmed down, simplified or even removed altogether. As an example, being able to cut recruitment or induction time would mean that new people could be up to speed and making a contribution faster than ever before. This would produce visible and measurable benefits which would be felt across the whole business; a real demonstration of alignment.

Conclusions

All good words and intentions account for nothing if you fail to deliver. As Benjamin Franklin said, "Well done is better than well said." As People Professionals, you'll need to do all that you can to ensure that you deliver flawlessly at all times.

Although the Germans are recognised word wide for excellence in engineering, July 27 1994 was a landmark day for Porsche. Despite what you may think about the brand now, this date represents the first Porsche Carrera to come off the production line without any defects! The efforts that Porsche put into flawless delivery were considerable, as were the benefits which they keep enjoying day after day.

The "doing" part of your role may not always be the sexiest, but it's the part that will deliver for your business and will demonstrate alignment. Focus on delivering the very best that you can at all times, reduce waste and empower your teams to deal with issues rather than passing them up the management chain of command.

Flawless execution can take years to achieve—indeed, for some businesses it may not be achieved—but you must never stop trying to make the necessary improvements.

Chapter 9: Activities

For this chapter I suggest that you review the manner in which you execute within your business. Ask yourself each of the following questions and consider how you would address any shortfall.

- Do you always deliver to meet expectations? Do you achieve this every time? If not, what could you do that would make a real difference?
- Are your front line teams really empowered to deal with issues, or do they have to refer issues up the management chain? If they're not empowered then what can you do to resolve this? What benefits would your business enjoy if your people were fully empowered? How much better would your business be?
- Are you doing all you can to improve productivity and remove excess waste? When was the last time you reviewed a process? What small steps are you making that will save your business time and money?

10

Talent, Leadership, Innovation, Mergers And Partnerships

"It's too easy, as a team grows, to put up with a few B players, and they then attract a few more B players, and soon you will even have some C players.

The Microsoft experience taught me that A players like to work only with other A players, which means you can't indulge B players."

Steve Jobs
Founder and CEO of Apple

Introduction

So far we've looked at the four key aspects which impact on your ability to create alignment within the People Profession. These are:

- strategy
- structure
- culture
- execution

If you recall, earlier I also said that great alignment came from two additional aspects from a variety of four. These were:

- talent
- leadership
- innovation
- mergers and partnerships

As a People Professional, you'll almost certainly argue that talent and leadership are key aspects for success, but let's look at each of these in more detail.

1. Talent

Over the past few years, the issue of talent has become a big issue amongst People Professionals. We've heard of the "talent time bomb" and the "war for talent", not to mention a number of other headline-grabbing statements, which all suggest that without the right talent or the right talent strategies businesses will fail. The truth though is exceptionally simple: better people make better businesses. It stands to reason, so let's not make it more complicated than it needs to be.

According to Wikipedia, talent management is "The anticipation of required human capital the organization needs at the time then setting a plan to meet those needs." How simple is that? It's worth noting that the terms "talent" and "talent management" can mean different things to different businesses. For some it's about the management of high-worth individuals—"the talented"—while for others it's about how talent is managed generally—i.e. on the assumption that all people have talent which should be identified and liberated.

Top flight football clubs, for example, regularly go all out to secure talent with major new signings bringing headline news and eye-watering wages. According to the book "Soccernomics" by Simon Kuper and Stefan Szymanski, the majority of talent transfers in football just don't work because many of the clubs expect their new, highly-paid employee to get on with their life even though they could be in a foreign country, speak little of the language and have virtually no local friends. Football talent is therefore well understood, but perhaps not always managed appropriately.

Film and design companies are also clearly searching for the best possible talent. Look at the average blockbuster and you'll almost certainly see a great list of talent on the credits. After all, who really wants to see a film full of nobodies? Of course there are films that break this mould, such as Alan Parker's "The Commitments", but these are few and far between.

Design houses and architect practices are also keen to have the right talent leading their business. Indeed it is this talent that will actually make the business its money. Rogers Stirk Harbour + Partners is led by Richard Rogers, who is perhaps best known for his work on the Pompidou Centre, the Lloyd's building and Millennium Dome. Foster + Partners is led by Norman Foster, whose breakthrough building was arguably the Willis Building in Ipswich. He has since designed landmark structures such as Wembley Stadium and 30 St Mary Axe, more commonly known as The Gherkin. These businesses would not be what they are today without their key talent.

For most People Professionals the drive for the best talent is a little more down to earth. Of course businesses do compete for good talent but I'd argue that it's not quite at the level of the football clubs, film studios or design companies. Naturally you'll want the best talent possible within your business. After all, recruiting or developing poor talent is a sure-fire way of failing to achieve alignment.

"Talent", "top talent", "high potentials"—businesses use different words for what is essentially the same thing, but where do you begin to find the talent of the future? There's been a huge amount written on the subject of talent, especially within the past ten years. I'd like to say that there's a magic formula but the book "Moneyball: The Art of Winning an Unfair Game" by Michael Lewis changed my mind on this. Michael's book tells the story of the Oakland Athletics baseball team and its general manager, Billy Beane. As the book unfolds, Billy ditches the decades-old approach of scouting for talent and begins to build a cost-effective team using analytical and evidence-based statistics. It's a gripping read and is now a film starring Brad Pitt. The "Moneyball" approach is quietly being adopted by top flight football teams who are looking more and more at the statistical performance of footballers.

For most People Professionals, however, you're not going to be able to assess the statistical performance of your team or that of potential new members. When recruiting or promoting trainers you'll be able to look at the scores on their feedback sheets as an indication of performance, but for the most part these are pretty meaningless (as we'll see in another chapter).

When faced with "traditional" ways of acquiring talent, I'd like to suggest you follow these four key rules:

- promote from within whenever possible,
- make sure you have access to the very best training programmes,
- design jobs that will intrigue and attract your best performers, and
- become personally involved in winning the war for talent.

Promote from within whenever possible

There's almost nothing worse than working hard for a business for a number of years only to see someone brought in above you from outside. If it happens once then fine, but if it's a reoccurring theme then current talent is unlikely to stay. Filling high-end roles with internal people signals a number of things. It signals that the business has:

- good people that it's keen to promote,
- spotted good talent at an early stage, and
- developed talent to take on the high-end roles.

Naturally there will be times when external candidates are best; perhaps you're developing something new and need rapid access to expertise, but try and make this the exception. Good people are more likely to stay with you if they see a path to the top roles. One client I work with can demonstrate that around forty percent of their very top jobs are occupied by people who joined the company as apprentices. Because there's such a clear path to the top, key talent is retained.

Make sure you have access to the very best training programmes

Promoting people from within is best, but you can't expect people to develop all on their own. Just as the top athletes all have top coaches, so you should also ensure that your talent has access to the very best training programmes. This doesn't mean that your business has to develop these training programmes, but it must ensure it has access to the very best. For top managers this may mean getting them on advanced management programmes at the best business schools. For specialists (recruiters, learning designers etc.) there will be a need to make sure they have access to the very best, publicly available programmes. We all like someone to take a proactive interest in our development and by providing access to the very best training programmes, you'll be going the extra mile to secure talent for the future.

Design jobs that will intrigue and attract your best performers

I suspect that many of us, at some point in our working lives, have undertaken a mundane or boring job. Perhaps it was a Saturday job in a retail store, perhaps a gap-year job, or perhaps a first step on the employment ladder. Either way you'll remember just what a mind-numbing time you had! To develop and retain your very best talent you'll need an environment that is highly challenging and rewarding. Make sure you use your talent to help make key decisions and run the business rather than just letting a few people make all the decisions. Involve people, give them responsibility and authority, ask your teams to develop new ideas and solutions and make sure it's a team effort. Scott Page's book "The Difference" shows the benefit that can be gained by using people from different backgrounds to solve problems. That doesn't just mean ethnic or gender differences, it means putting programmers with graphic designers, with programme managers, with HR business partners and so on to solve problems. Mash-up your teams; it'll make the working environment much more engaging and will help retain your talent. It'll also be a great way of spotting talent for the future. After all, the famous Sugar Puffs "Honey Monster" adverts were created by a chemist, so talent can be generated from all areas of your business.

Become personally involved in winning the war for talent

As a People Professional you'll need to get your hands dirty in order to identify and develop the best talent. That means you'll need to do something other than sitting behind a desk! Cruel words I know, but talent will not always be found by putting an advert in the local paper. One creative company I worked with made a habit of attending the annual student show at the local art school. Here it would rapidly identify potential talent and would be able to talk freely about opportunities. The best talent was therefore identified early on and the cost of recruitment was virtually zero. Do you attend conferences and exhibitions or read articles to identify talent? If not, then you should. Watching someone present at a conference and talking to them afterwards will reveal more than an interview ever would—and it's virtually free.

Having a personal interest in the talent you recruit also creates a personal responsibility to see that talent looked after and developed in the right way. What better buzz can there be than to see someone progress in a business while knowing that "I spotted them, y'know!"

2. Leadership

As each of the key headings in this chapter shows, there's just so much that's been written about leadership over the years that I'd be foolish to try and repeat it all here. As a high-level checklist, and according to Santa Clara University and the Tom Peters Group, the following are traits of a good leader:

- **Honest**—Display sincerity, integrity, and candour in all your actions. Deceptive behaviour will not inspire trust.
- **Competent**—Base your actions on reason and moral principles. Do not make decisions based on childlike emotional desires or feelings.
- **Forward-looking**—Set goals and have a vision of the future. The vision must be owned throughout the organisation. Effective leaders envision what they want and how to get it. They habitually pick priorities stemming from their basic values.

- **Inspiring**—Display confidence in all that you do. By showing endurance in mental, physical, and spiritual stamina, you will inspire others to reach for new heights. Take charge when necessary.
- **Intelligent**—Read, study, and seek challenging assignments.
- **Fair-minded**—Show fair treatment to all people. Prejudice is the enemy of justice. Display empathy by being sensitive to the feelings, values, interests, and well-being of others.
- **Broad-minded**—Seek out diversity.
- **Courageous**—Have the perseverance to accomplish a goal, regardless of the seemingly insurmountable obstacles. Display a confident calmness when under stress.
- **Straightforward**—Use sound judgment to make good decisions at the right time.
- **Imaginative**—Make timely and appropriate changes in your thinking, plans, and methods. Show creativity by thinking of new and better goals, ideas, and solutions to problems. Be innovative!

While the above are personal traits, let's look at two critical skills that People Professionals should acquire which will actively demonstrate leadership within their businesses; leadership that will show you understand the business and will enable alignment. The two skills are:

- strengthening relationships with everyone in your business, and
- spotting opportunities and problems early on.

Strengthening relationships with everyone in your business

Relationships are the life-blood of any business. In Chapter 7 we looked at the benefits of promoting co-operation and the exchange of information with the emphasis on the way in which actively pursuing these aims can really strengthen your alignment. As People Professionals you should do all you can to build and strengthen your relationships with everyone in your business; that's **everyone**. Don't just focus on the senior management, the "Top Team" (or whatever it's called in your business). Talk to everyone about what they're doing and also about what you can do to help. It stands to reason that the more people you talk to, the more you'll learn about the business. You'll discover what senior managers **really** think the issues are, what they **really** feel about the services you're providing and what challenges they are particularly focusing on for the future. You'll also hear from the people on the front line about the challenges they face and the issues they need to address. By strengthening relationships you'll inevitably discover invaluable information which will assist you with alignment.

Spotting problems and opportunities early on

When you're really aligned within a business you'll be talking to people at all levels, sharing information and really having your finger on the pulse. You'll also be in touch with what's happening in the outside world and will have well-developed radar to sense issues that may affect your business. The ability to spot problems early on and begin to fix them will amply demonstrate to senior managers that you know what's what. Just as you're spotting problems, you'll also be spotting opportunities and again your senior management will thank you for this.

But what happens when the problems or opportunities aren't spotted, or aren't spotted in time? I've mentioned this story earlier in the book but Nick Buckles, head of G4S, the world's largest security company, failed to keep his finger on the pulse. Responsible for providing security to the London 2012 Olympic Games, Nick decided (with just two weeks to go before the official opening ceremony) to see how things were progressing. The rest is well documented. G4S failed to provide the security cover for which they were contracted. The police and military had to cover off the shortfall in manpower and the company may end up losing £50m from the £284m contract as a result of the fiasco. Two directors lost their jobs and the long-term reputational damage is unknown, but the impact to G4S of failing to spot issues early on is clear.

3. Innovation

Within businesses, innovation is all about creating better or more effective products, processes, services or technologies. Innovation, invention and improvement are often used interchangeably within businesses; however, it's worth taking a moment to distinguish between them. Innovation differs from invention in that innovation refers to the use of a better idea or method, whereas invention refers more directly to the creation of the idea or method itself. Innovation differs from improvement in that innovation refers to the notion of doing something different—from the Latin innovare: "to change" rather than doing the same thing better.

Apple is widely considered to be one of the most innovative companies on the planet. Did it invent the graphical user interface? No, Apple 'borrowed' it from Xerox and made it better. Did it invent the MP3 player? No, it improved upon designs already in the market. Did it invent the smartphone? No, it improved on concepts and products already in use. In truth, Apple has invented very little, but innovated more than most. As People Professionals the opportunity for you to invent a new psychometric test or a new e-learning system would be rare. However, the opportunity for you to innovate on what's already in the market is enormous and taking this approach can bring immense and long-term benefits to your business and clearly demonstrate your alignment to future success.

The world's fifty most innovative companies

Businessweek collaborated with Boston Consulting Group to publish its 2010 list of the fifty most innovative companies in the world based on a survey of corporate executives. There's been considerable movement in the list from previous years although Apple retains a firm grip on the top spot. China with four entries, India with two and South Korea with three have all increased their showing. Britain has four entries—Virgin, BSkyB, Vodafone and HSBC. Germany has three companies in the list and France has none. Here's the list:

Rank	Company	Country
1	Apple	US
2	Google	US

3	Microsoft	US
4	IBM	US
5	Toyota Motor	Japan
6	Amazon.com	US
7	LG Electronics	South Korea
8	BYD	China
9	General Electric	US
10	Sony	Japan
11	Samsung Electronics	South Korea
12	Intel	US
13	Ford Motor	US
14	Research In Motion	Canada
15	Volkswagen	Germany
16	Hewlett-Packard	US
17	Tata Group	India
18	BMW	Germany
19	Coca-Cola	US
20	Nintendo	Japan
21	Wal-Mart Stores	US
22	Hyundai Motor	South Korea
23	Nokia	Finland
24	Virgin Group	Britain
25	Proctor & Gamble	US
26	Honda Motor	Japan
27	Fast Retailing	Japan
28	Haier Electronics	China
29	McDonalds	US
30	Lenovo	China
31	Cisco Systems	US
32	Walt Disney	US
33	Reliance Industries	India
34	Siemens	Germany
35	Dell	US

36	Nestlé	Switzerland
37	British Sky Broadcasting	Britain
38	Vodafone	Britain
39	JP Morgan Chase	US
40	Oracle	US
41	Petronas	Brazil
42	Banco Santander	Spain
43	Fiat	Italy
44	China Mobile	China
45	Goldman Sachs	US
46	Nike	US
47	HTC	Taiwan
48	Facebook	US
49	HSBC	Britain
50	Verizon Communications	US

The methodology behind this survey is highly subjective and depends on what the survey group perceives as "innovative". However, reputations matter and this list provides a powerful indication of the businesses which are innovating more than most.

As a People Professional, constant innovation is a must. As we've discussed earlier, standing still is not an option and the need to continually refresh and improve upon everything you do is essential to maintain alignment.

4. Mergers and partnerships

Rarely can a business achieve everything it wants on its own. Changes in economic outlook, technologies, manpower requirements and regional boundaries can all create the need for mergers and partnerships. Most large businesses today have a number of "strategic partners" who provide essential support. IBM and Cisco have formed a "strategic alliance" and Cisco has strategic partnerships with businesses such as Hitachi, CSC and Capgemini.

Partnerships are an essential ingredient of modern day life and allow businesses to manage more readily elements of their operations and also join together with other businesses to serve bigger and more diverse customers. The 2012 London Olympics is a great case in point. EDF Energy provided the electricity; the cars came from BMW, communications infrastructure from BT and money transmission services from Lloyds TSB. Without these partners, the Olympics could not have been the success it ultimately was.

Within the People Profession there are strategic partnerships which exist with recruitment agencies, e-learning companies, universities and business schools and even hotel chains, all providing appropriate locations and services for meetings, training sessions and conferences. Partnerships are an excellent way for People Professionals to extend their reach and develop capability. Should you need to produce a series of corporate videos, develop a range of e-learning courses for new entrants, or source long-term executive education, then partnerships are an excellent way of addressing these issues with a minimum of fuss or additional investment. But a word of warning: just as you'd spend time courting and getting to know a future life partner, so it should be with a potential business partner.

Take time to understand your potential partner and make sure their values align with your own. Wherever possible, look as far ahead as you can to predict the partners you'll need and then formalise this partnership at a time when you least need them. This may sound strange at first, but trying to agree terms for a partnership when there's business and time pressures can only make for bad decisions. Take your time and have your partners lined up for when you really need them. Value your partners and don't just change them for the sake of it. Some businesses do this every few years just because they feel it will drive lower costs, but it rarely does. Work together with your partners and over the longer-term you'll both reap the benefits.

The ability to identify and nurture key partners is an essential skill and one that will allow you to rapidly develop competence in new areas. Good partners can also assist you with safety and security by providing additional services in times of rapid business growth, or by handling key elements of your business during times of difficulty. Examples could be the use of recruitment companies to enable you to cope during times of rapid expansion, or the use of specialist employment lawyers who seek to protect your business should it come under threat from disgruntled ex-employees.

Although you should work hard to nurture your partners, you should also realise that a partnership may not last forever. Changing business needs and the ability of your partner to meet these will inevitably bring some partnerships to an end.

Unlike partnerships, which are not necessarily permanent, mergers (sometimes called acquisitions) most certainly are! Businesses have been merging for years as part of creating wealth and dominating markets. Economic history has been divided into "Merger Waves" based on the merger activities in the business world as:

Period	Wave	Focus
1897-1904	First	Horizontal mergers
1916-1929	Second	Vertical mergers
1965-1969	Third	Diversified conglomerate mergers
1981-1989	Fourth	Congeneric mergers, hostile takeovers, corporate raiding
1992-2000	Fifth	Cross-border mergers
2003-2008	Sixth	Shareholder activism, private equity, leveraged buy-outs

As People Professionals you're unlikely to be directly involved in the mechanics of mergers, such as identifying target businesses, financing and so on, but you'll certainly have a major role to play in helping to 'glue' a new business to an existing one.

It's worth noting that for many current mergers the buyers aren't necessarily hungry for the target business's hard assets. They tend to be more interested in acquiring thoughts, methodologies, people and relationships. Paul Graham recognised this in his 2005 essay "Hiring is Obsolete", where he was probably the first to identify the trend in which large companies such as Google, Yahoo! or Microsoft were choosing to acquire start-ups instead of hiring new recruits to develop their businesses. Today, companies are being bought for their patents, licences, market share, name brand, research staff, methods, customer base, or culture. When a CEO wants to boost corporate performance or jump-start long-term growth, the thought of merging with another company can be extraordinarily attractive. Indeed, companies spend more than $2 trillion on acquisitions every year. Yet study after study puts the failure rate of mergers and acquisitions somewhere between seventy and ninety percent.

It's worth noting that employee turnover is a major contributor to merger failures. Soft capital, like this, is very perishable, fragile and fluid. Integrating it usually takes more finesse and expertise than integrating machinery, real estate, inventory and other tangibles. The turnover in target businesses is double the turnover experienced in non-merged firms for the ten years following the merger. That's a lot of good people potentially walking out of the door! As a People Professional, your ability to make integration as seamless as possible will be absolutely essential to achieve alignment.

Conclusions

In this chapter we've looked at the additional aspects of our 4+2 recipe, which are:

- talent
- leadership
- innovation
- mergers and partnerships

As People Professionals, you'll need to demonstrate a capability within your business of at least two of the above in order to stand a chance of achieving alignment. The two areas which will help you best align will be wholly dependent on the type of business you're in. However, I'd suggest that no matter what the focus of your business, having some capability in **all** the above areas would be useful tools for every People Professional.

Chapter 10: Activities

It's a useful exercise for you to recap the key elements of this chapter and consider the needs of your own business.

I've already mentioned that all People Professionals should ideally have capabilities in all of the areas mentioned in this chapter, but there may be some areas where you feel you need to excel. Perhaps you're in a technology business where the need to manage mergers is critical to success, or perhaps your need to build partnerships is the key to long-term success. Either way, it's worth taking a few moments to think about how capable you are in each of these areas and consider any development you may need to reach your ideal level of competence.

11

Measuring The People Profession

"The only man who behaves sensibly is my tailor; he takes my measurements anew every time he sees me, while all the rest go on with their old measurements and expect me to fit them."

George Bernard Shaw
Irish playwright and a co-founder of the London School of Economics

Introduction

There's an old management mantra that states "What gets measured gets managed." This is also akin to the saying "If you can't measure it, you can't manage it." Either way, it's clear that having some form of metrics, measures or KPIs can be a good thing. When he was at Princeton, Einstein had a sign hanging over his office which read, "Not everything that counts can be counted, and not everything that can be counted counts." As Einstein suggested, it's possible to measure the wrong things and I believe that within the People Profession we're in danger of measuring the unnecessary. We're doing this in an unproductive way and sadly we don't know we're actually doing it! Even more sadly, we make 'business' decisions on the back of incomplete information. We have to measure the right moments and act upon the results accordingly rather than blindly accepting various results without question.

In this chapter we'll take a tour through the world of people metrics and KPIs, paying special interest to the way in which people outcomes are measured and assessed.

Painful experiences

Let's start with a story. For a number of years I worked within an organisation where, with hindsight (which is always easy to do), we were focusing on and measuring the wrong things! When I joined the organisation we were trying to raise the profile of the training department (as they were called in those days) because we wanted people to take us more seriously in order to gain a greater slice of the limited corporate resources. We believed that money meant more courses, which meant more success.

One of the measures bandied about the industry in those days was the 'average number of training days per employee.' A "leader" in this field at the time was IBM who provided (from memory) an average of eight training days per year per employee. The company I was working with felt that this was the "holy grail" of training measures and unless we delivered eight training days per employee per year then we were doomed to failure. And clearly eight **had** to be the magic number because after all, IBM was hugely successful, and we thought this was **because** of all the training it provided to its employees. We thought that if only we could provide as much training as IBM, we too would be a hugely successful organisation. This all sounds rather strange now but trust me, this **was** the key issue many years ago!

We now know that this logic just doesn't hold true. There are many reasons why organisations prosper and providing a set number of training days per employee may not be such a great measure after all. Perhaps the amount of training provided **could** be a measure of success, but it could also be a measure of how complex the products are, or how dim the employees are (unlikely), or indeed for a whole host of other reasons. And for those reasons it's of course a totally meaningless measure but we focused on this as well as measuring the amount of money spent on training per employee. We were naïve, but we were happy!

I don't propose to go on and on and on about these measures, but needless to say I **don't** feel they are measures of effectiveness or value, rather they are input metrics (more of these later). Let's stand back for a moment and think—what the heck **is** a training day anyway? Is it seven hours or eight hours? Do two half-day sessions really add up to a one-day session? What if someone's done some e-learning? Should that be measured in elapsed time, or should we measure it some other way because we 'feel' e-learning is a more efficient way of training?

It's a sad but true fact that, for a period of time, I actually thought these were the most important things; but no longer. Now I realise they are not a real measure of the effectiveness of the People Profession—certainly not when taken on their own; they are just input metrics and therefore only give us a small element of the overall picture. And this is where the challenge begins.

As People Professionals we **have** to get away from measuring "things" and "perceived costs" and start measuring **value** delivered to the business. We have to begin measuring the 'right moments'.

Unfortunately, this is not likely to happen any time soon. The Chartered Institute of Personnel and Development (CIPD) publish an annual Learning and Talent Development Survey which, even this year (2012), states that:

> "The median number of training hours employees receive per year is 24 (among those who track the data). This suggests a decrease on previous years (2011: 5 days median, 2010: 4 days median, 2009: 5 days median). Size and sector of organisation had no significant impact on the median amount of training per employee."

This is a totally meaningless measure and it's a real shame that the CIPD, as a major professional organisation, focuses on these moments. To be brutally honest, as long as the CIPD continues to report these moments others will follow, assuming that they're adopting 'best practice'.

And shock, horror—the CIPD is not alone! The BBC claims that, via its Academy, it delivers over 57,000 days of training each year to both BBC staff and the wider broadcasting industry. Given that the BBC employs about 23,000 staff and assuming (for the purposes of this exercise) that it **only** trains BBC staff then this represents fewer than 2.5 days per employee per year. That's fifty percent **less** than the CIPD median—and we're talking about the most respected broadcaster on the planet. See what I mean—a totally meaningless moment!

Take a long hard look at your business. Never mind how big your budget is, the question **always** has to be how much value are you adding? Industry thought leader Jay Cross agrees. He says that: "The best proof is the link between your learning initiatives and your business results."

I agree totally and continuing on this theme, here's something that could really get you sweating.

If you're using Kirkpatrick to measure learning and development—STOP.

If you're trying to measure return on investment (ROI) STOP—for now.

I'm not about to blatantly rubbish various well-established approaches for the sake of it, but I **do** want to take you on a journey so you can **really** understand the benefit your work is bringing to your organisation, rather than just spouting out the same old people-metrics, day after day. To make this chapter easily digestible, I've divided it into two parts. If you're a novice (or you just want a refresher) then read both parts; if you feel you already know about data, metrics, KPIs and so on then jump straight to part II.

So let's begin our journey . . . .

Part I: Everything you wanted to know about people moments, but were afraid to ask

Let's begin by defining some of the terms with which we'll be working. You may use slightly different definitions within your business; however, the following will allow a clear explanation of the issues at play. Let's start at the very beginning by looking at data sources.

Data sources

Data sources are the places where you get your basic numbers. These are places such as databases, spreadsheets, feedback forms, observations and so on. Your HR system would most likely be the source for data about employees, your sales system the source of data regarding sales for your various products and so on. Take a moment to think about all the data sources within your business. Not all data will be held in systems; some will be written on scraps of paper, on spreadsheets and even in people's heads. Oh . . . and you also need to consider whether you actually have access to them, or if the information is generally out of your reach.

Data

As mentioned, data can exist in a variety of forms: as numbers, or text on pieces of paper, as bits and bytes stored in electronic memory, or as facts stored in a person's mind. Above all, data is collection of facts, such as values or measurements. For the purposes of this chapter, data is the lowest level of granularity of information that we need, e.g. the number of people in your organisation or the number of people who are registered with your learning management system.

Metrics

Metrics is the term we use when we're referring to a direct numerical measure that represents a piece of business data to which we can refer in one or more dimensions. Sounds all technical, but don't worry, it's not that difficult! An example would be "induction courses per year". In this case, the measure would be the total number of induction courses delivered (data) and the dimension would be time (year).

For any given piece of data, you may also want to see alternative metric views. For instance, you may want to see the number of induction courses per day, per week or per month.

As People Professionals, you're almost certainly familiar with a number of common metrics such as staff turnover per year, number of e-learning courses delivered per week, number of successful test completions per year and so on. The potential for metrics is all around us and we can create (should we so wish) a plethora of these, some of which may add value but many of which will not . . . but let's not get too ahead of ourselves for now!

Delta

Delta is represented by the symbol Δ (the Greek letter delta). The delta is the **change** in a metric between two known points, e.g. if you recruited 100 people in month one and 120 people in month two then the delta between month one and month two would be 20.

Knowing the delta for a given metric allows us an additional factor of analysis and is frequently used to denote a change in time, velocity, quantity, or acceleration. In the above example we can express the delta (20) as a percentage, so we can say that in month two we recruited 20% more people than in month one. This doesn't mean that the people you've recruited are necessarily any good, or that they're going to add value within your business, but we can definitely say that we recruited 20% more people!

Indicators

Indicators are the compound result of calculations which use a number of metrics. Let's take an example: you may have 1000 people who start an e-learning course in a year, but in order to calculate the number of people who failed to complete the e-learning course in the same year, you need to subtract the number of successful course completions (perhaps calculated as a result of passing a test) from the number of people who originally registered for the course. So if 1000 people registered in a year and only 800 passed the course, the failure rate would be 1000 minus 800, or 200 people. We can either express this as a number (200) or as a percentage of the people who registered (200/1000 x 100 = 20%). So the percentage of people who registered for the e-learning course and failed to complete it would be 20%. We can also reverse the above example to show successes rather than failures. So for the above example, there would have been an 80% success rate, i.e. 80% of the people who registered for the e-learning course in a particular year actually completed it.

Indicators are **very** useful in showing us the bigger picture, e.g. percentage of passes or failures etc. As we'll see later, these are not the be-all and end-all of measuring meaningful people moments, but they're a good start.

Key performance indicators (KPIs)

And now to the dreaded KPI! A KPI is simply a measure that is tied to a target. Most often, a KPI represents how far a measure is above or below a pre-determined target. KPIs are usually shown as a percentage of actual performance compared to the target and are designed to let a business know instantly if they are on or off their plan without having to focus consciously on the measures being represented. Let's look at an example:

A business may decide that in order to hit its quarterly sales target it needs to sell £10,000 of widgets per week. The measure would be widget sales per week; the target would be £10,000. If we used a percentage to represent this KPI and we had sold £8,000 of widgets by Wednesday, the business would see that they were at 80% of their target. Many businesses also add a RAG indicator (red, amber or green) to their KPIs to provide a visual indication of how close or far away they are from the desired target.

Putting your KPIs into tiers

Having selected appropriate KPIs, businesses will often group them into tiers, with tier one being the most important indicators of success; tier two KPIs supporting tier one and tier three KPIs supporting tier two. Let's look at an example:

A people function may have a wide range of KPIs, but we'll look at how one set may fit together. At the tier one level you may well have "Percentage of Learners Reaching Competence within Target Time". This KPI would apply to **all** programmes across a business. The tier two KPIs could well have the same focus but apply to different programmes, e.g. compliance, sales, induction etc. The tier three KPIs would again focus on reaching competence, but would apply to each of the courses that makes up a particular programme. For example, within the compliance programme you may well have courses on data protection, anti-bribery, anti-money laundering and so on.

The construction and arrangement of your KPIs allows you not only to see the high-level 'rolled-up' moments, but you also have the ability to 'drill down' through each of the tiers to examine any areas of poor performance.

The downside of metrics and KPIs

Metrics and KPIs are great for monitoring your business, but what would you do if your metrics were revealing performance that was 50% below target? Would you be able to explain in a rational manner why this is a problem for your business? Would you know the cost of this poor performance? Would you know where to start looking for possible causes? Would you know what to do in order to address a performance shortfall? What would you do if people began to manipulate your metrics and KPIs for their own reward? Would you have a set of 'wobble board' metrics so that as one metric changed for the better, others would show a negative impact to indicate they were being manipulated? No? Well perhaps you should think about this. Unfortunately, as soon as KPIs are introduced as a measure of reward they **will** be abused. This is known as a perverse incentive, which is an incentive that has an unintended and undesirable result, contrary to the interests of the incentive makers. Perverse incentives have dogged KPIs for centuries. Let's look at a few examples:

- In Hanoi, under French colonial rule, a programme paying people a bounty for each rat pelt handed in to the authorities was intended to exterminate rats. Instead, it led to the farming of rats for profit.

- Funding fire departments by the number of fires attended is meant to reward the fire departments that do the most work. However, it may discourage them from fire prevention activities, which reduce the overall number of fires.

- 19th century palaeontologists travelling to China used to pay peasants for each fragment of dinosaur bone that they found. They later discovered that the peasants dug up the bones and then smashed them into many pieces, greatly reducing their scientific value in order to maximise their payments.

- In 1696, the English parliament adopted a tax under which dwellings were to be assessed according to the number of windows. Although the tax was intended to be progressive in that it exempted houses with fewer than ten windows from the bulk of the assessment, in operation it exacerbated the gap in living conditions between rich and poor as landlords were incentivised to brick up tenement windows to reduce their tax liability, leaving working-class tenants with insufficient light and ventilation.

- Architects and engineers are often paid a percentage fee according to the total amount spent on a project. This, however, can lead to excessively costly projects and expensive overruns.

- Within the National Health Service (NHS), hospitals are able to claim money for each test, treatment and referral. Surprise, surprise, lots of treatments are provided, but there's no focus on the overall health benefits. Sadly, people with medically unexplained abdominal symptoms are three times more likely to have their gallbladder removed, twice as likely to have their appendix or uterus removed and one and a half times more likely to have back surgery compared with a matched control group. They are also significantly more likely to commit suicide after surgery.

The upside of metrics and KPIs

Although KPIs can be manipulated in such a way as to have a negative impact on your business, they can also add real and lasting value. KPIs can add a focus to your business and allow you to see the results of the work you're doing. They can also be a good way of demonstrating benefit to others. So before we move away from KPIs for now, for each one you develop make sure you ask yourself, "What value does improving this KPI bring to my business?" Some KPIs are blindingly obvious, others are less so, but if you can't see the benefit then neither will anyone else.

Concluding Part I

You have now concluded Part I of this chapter where you've taken a tour through the foundation elements of measures. You've looked at data and deltas and indicators and metrics and even the dreaded KPIs. You've also looked at the upside and downside of metrics. In the second part of this chapter we'll finish our journey by looking at how metrics and KPIs are used to evaluate and determine performance of people programmes and as we'll see, things are not always as clear-cut as they could be!

Part II: Making sense of all those numbers

You may recall that in Part I I mentioned these rather blunt challenges:

"If you're using Kirkpatrick to measure
learning and development—STOP"

and

"If you're trying to measure Return on Investment (ROI)
STOP—for now"

I guess it's now time for me to explain where I'm coming from. Part I covered the background to data, metrics, indicators and KPIs. Having covered some ground rules, let's look more closely at the impact of metrics and measures on the people landscape.

Evaluation vs. Performance

For many People Professionals there is a major confusion between "evaluation" and "performance". For the most part, as we shall see, People Professionals use evaluation metrics, but treat them as though they were performance metrics. This is not only a big mistake, it is the source of many deep-rooted issues whereby businesses view the People Profession with disdain because they keep banging on about "happy sheets" rather than talking about real business benefits. So let's see how you can start to make things better.

Let's start by refocusing your 'map of the world'

The first part of your journey of change is to begin to refocus your 'map of the world'. If your map is mainly based on "happy sheet" metrics then you need to look again at what you measure, together with the weight and reliance you place on each measure. For People Professionals I'm suggesting that you begin by assigning your metrics, indicators and KPIs to one of **three** key categories. These are:

- input metrics
- process metrics, and
- output metrics (you may also refer to these as 'outcome' or 'results' metrics).

You may describe the above differently within your business, but for the purposes of this chapter I'll be using the above terms, which you can interpret as appropriate. Let's begin by looking at input metrics.

Input metrics

These are metrics that **drive** your people function. Examples that you may well recognise include:

- number of staff trained,
- staff turnover,

- staff absence and sickness,
- number of courses on offer (or within your learning management system),
- number of attendees (or registered delegates) per course,
- cost of courses (either purchased outright or pay per delegate),
- cost of other resources (rooms, network costs, hosting etc.)

Despite what many People Professionals think, input metrics do **not** show value for the organisation. Let me give you some examples.

I've often been privileged to judge the Learning Awards which are organised by the Learning and Performance Institute (LPI). Year after year, businesses try to win their award category by quoting input metrics and **only** input metrics. They make statements such as "Last year we trained seven hundred staff in underwater knitting and this was a twenty percent increase compared with the number of people we trained the year before." Hmmmm . . . but so what?

Input metrics (on their own) do not demonstrate a business's success; they merely show a level of activity and associated cost. As we'll see later, input metrics can provide some very useful information, but they do not provide the information that you really want to hold up to your senior managers as demonstrating value. More about this later, but first let's take a look at process metrics.

Process metrics

These are metrics which measure your internal processes. They're great for making sure your people function is operating effectively. Examples may include:

- number of joining instructions sent (usually via email these days),
- number of joining instructions accepted (you can also use number of course registrations),
- number of staff interviewed for new roles, quality of training venue (more about this later),

- quality of food at training venue (more about this later too),
- quality of trainer (and oh, so **much more** about this later), and
- amount of learning that occurred. Guess what? Yes, more of this later!

As with input metrics, process metrics (on their own) **do not** show value for a business; what they do provide is an indication of the effectiveness of your internal processes, and little else. Keeping an eye on your process metrics allows you (for the most part) to ensure that key delivery elements are working according to plan.

Output metrics

As mentioned earlier, I've called these "output metrics" because they're the output of all the effort from your people function. You may also call them "outcome" or "results" metrics.

The actual metrics used will depend on your business and the key issues you're trying to address. That said, some of your output metrics may well include:

- increase in sales performance,
- increase in safety performance,
- reduction in errors,
- increase in profits, or
- increase in retained customers etc.

Output metrics are those metrics which are the output (or results) of the effort you've provided to your business. I'll talk later about how you can align these to the work you're doing, but for now just know that, as output metrics, these should be the key measures within your business.

Putting it all together

Input metrics show the level of activity within your people function, but little else. Let's take an input metric and work through the issues. For our example, let's take the imaginary metric "Number of people trained in essential compliance".

Let's begin by assuming that last year your business trained 1,000 people in "essential compliance", and this year they've trained 1,200 people in the same subject. That's an increase year-on-year of 200 people trained so that **must** be good, eh? Well maybe, but not necessarily. What this metric shows is merely the level of supply for any one course or programme. It does **not** show how many people registered for the course but could not get a place, or how many registered for the course and did not complete it, or indeed how many people the organisation **should** have trained in order to keep pace with their business needs, or whether in fact they need to train any at all, or whether they should have been training them in some other topic instead.

Taking the example above (and using some of the techniques mentioned in Part I), the delta for the "essential compliance" course between one year and the next is 200 (1200-1000). This represents a 20% increase between one year and the next. On first assessment this looks like a 'good' result; I mean, a 20% improvement on anything year-on-year must be good in this day and age—surely?

But wait a minute. Although 1,200 people were trained, what was the **demand** from the business? After all, delivering 1,200 courses to your business if the demand was for 1,800 courses suddenly isn't that good. And if the demand **was** for 1,800 courses, this means that 600 people potentially went without critical training. So rather than celebrating a 20% improvement you should really be mourning a 50% shortfall! Having any form of isolated measure can be exceptionally dangerous; you should always have some comparison or relevance to add meaning. Here's an amusing example:

Friend to Groucho Marx: *"Life is difficult!"*

Marx to friend: *"Compared to what?"*

Although the above example didn't give you the result you potentially wanted, it could, if looked at differently, have given you a whole host of important information that would be critical to the success of your offering. Let's look again at the business's demand for 1,800 "essential compliance" courses per year.

If we are to assume that delivering 1,800 "essential compliance" courses is the **right** level for a business, and assuming that each course delivery costs £100 per person, then from this information we can derive all manner of additional useful information. We can, for example, extrapolate the above information to provide:

- total projected costs per year (£100 x 1,800 = £180,000)
- average number of courses per month (1,800 / 12 = 150)
- average cost of course per month (150 x £100 = £15,000)

This information is an exceptionally useful aid to planning. Knowing issues such as cost and volume allows you to prepare and flex your business accordingly. It also enables you to make some useful operational decisions, e.g. the impact of changes in key inputs. Let's look at a couple of examples.

If the "essential compliance" course was externally supplied and the cost was rising from £100 to £110 per person, then the following would apply:

- total projected costs per year (£110 x 1,800 = £198,000)
- increased costs year-on-year = £18,000, which is 10%
- number of courses to be delivered at current budget (£180,000 / £110 = 1636)
- shortfall of courses if budget remains fixed (1,800 - 1,636 = 164)
- percentage shortfall of courses (164 / 1,800 x 100 = 9.1%)

OK, let's now look at what promises to be some really controversial approaches as we look in more detail at process metrics.

I've already mentioned some of the classic people metrics, most of which are fairly self-evident. However, I'd like to take a closer look at the metrics surrounding 'good trainer' or 'amount learned' etc. These are classic level 1 and level 2 metrics which are often associated with the Kirkpatrick evaluation model and as a result are widely adopted within the learning and development community worldwide.

As a People Professional, you'll almost certainly know all about the Kirkpatrick evaluation model, which is based upon evaluating learning on four levels. These are:

1. Reaction: this measures how delegates felt about the training or learning,
2. Learning: this measures the increase of knowledge from before to after,
3. Behaviour: this is the extent that the learning is applied back in the workplace,
4. Results: the effect on the business or environment.

Donald Kirkpatrick (the originator of the model) is Emeritus Professor of the University of Wisconsin in North America and a past president of the American Society for Training and Development (ASTD). He is best known for creating this influential model of training evaluation. Kirkpatrick's ideas were first published in 1959, in a series of articles in the *US Training and Development Journal* but are better known from a book he published in 1975 entitled "Evaluating Training Programs".

The Kirkpatrick model has been around for many years (longer, I suspect, than many of you reading this book) and as such has become rather embedded in the "how we do things around here" approach of many People Professionals. Although I'm not setting out to rubbish this model, I would like to give you a very different slant on the adoption (or otherwise) of the Kirkpatrick model within your business.

Kirkpatrick Level 1

Level 1 metrics are all about the "reaction" of the delegates to the learning, or the location, or the trainer. Now that all sounds fair and reasonable, but a variety of commentators and research shows that there is **little correlation** between learner reactions and measures of learning, or subsequent measures of changed behaviour (see later). It's been suggested that "satisfaction" is not necessarily related to good learning and sometimes learner discomfort is actually essential for success.

Mixed results may indicate that what is measured at the reaction level stage might be important and more focused reaction-level questionnaires may be more informative about the value of training. But even ignoring the negative research, stand back for a moment and ask yourself if you **really** believe that there's a direct link between someone's liking for a location, a trainer or a lesson and their long-term performance. Crazy eh, but given these facts, why on earth do we continue to use these metrics?

I believe (and I hasten to add it's just my belief) that these metrics provide the senior People Professionals with what can only be described as "comfort metrics". Ask someone to vote on how they felt about having root canal treatment (and yes, I **have** been there) and I suggest that most people would not rate it as a pleasurable experience. But does it matter? Of course not! What matters most are the outcomes and **not** the processes!

Let me give you a personal example. At the start of my career, I attended a training programme in London and was getting on very well with the main trainer. During the programme we split into smaller groups and I had to work with a new trainer. I was pilloried! I was brought down to earth with a bang in front of my peers. If I'd been asked to rate the trainer I would have been very severe. But that's not the issue. The issue is that I've **never** forgotten what was said to me that day and my current performance is as a direct result of the feedback I received all those years ago. I may not have liked the trainer but boy, it sure made a difference to my results!

Neil Rackham, the best-selling author of "SPIN Selling" was asked to assess his best trainers. Surprisingly, trainers with the worst feedback from the students were the ones who actually delivered better salespeople. Put simply, the Level 1 data was giving the **wrong** picture! And this is not just a one-off occurrence. Roger Chevalier, Vice President of Performance for Century 21 Real Estate found that there was very little correlation between level 1 evaluations and how well people performed in the field. Echoing those thoughts, Donald Taylor, Chairman of the Learning and Performance Institute, has said,

"When I was running a 17-room training centre in London, I noted the 3L effect (lunch-loos-liking). If there was something wrong with the lunch or the loos, the scores for the trainer were marked down, even if it was the same trainer, on the same course, in the same room. And no, it wasn't just that trainer having a bad day—all classroom scores were marked down."

I totally agree. From my personal experience of running learning and development departments and businesses over the years, the three F's were always critical to the way people reacted to your courses. The three F's were:

- food,
- facilities, and
- finish time.

Get these right and the feedback will be positive **regardless** of the learning or impact or anything else. And you know what? For years people departments have assumed that good level 1 feedback means that "good learning" has taken place, when in reality it's more likely to be a measure of the cleanliness of the toilets. Oh, we have so much more to learn. Level 1 of Kirkpatrick, therefore, doesn't work that well as a measure of successful people interventions so let's see if the Level 2 measures fare any better.

Kirkpatrick Level 2

Level 2 is all about learning. It's about finding out if the learner acquired knowledge as a result of undertaking the training. Guess what? Most, if not all, learners would say that they did learn something, surprise, surprise! I mean, why on earth do people attend training if it's not to do some learning?

I know that I'm being quite facetious, but bear with me. Assume for a moment that you're about to take a course entitled "A beginner's guide to nuclear physics". The chances are that as a beginner you'll know precious little about the subject. After all, if you knew about it you wouldn't be taking a beginner's course! Let's also assume that each learner has their knowledge tested at the beginning and end of the course. Do you think they'll increase their learning? Of course they will! And yet knowing this basic fact, i.e. if we tell someone something and then ask them a question about it, then we shouldn't be at all surprised if they remember some of it. But within the people function we feel that this "immediate remembering" is the same as actual learning and nothing could be further from the truth.

Stupidity of approach

Bear with me for a while longer as I ask you to take a look at a classic scene from Monty Python's film "The Holy Grail". We join the action as a peasant woman asks King Arthur who he is . . .

King Arthur: "I am your king."

Woman: "Well I didn't vote for you."

King Arthur: "You don't vote for kings."

Woman: "Well how'd you become king then?" [Angelic music plays . . .]

King Arthur: "The Lady of the Lake, her arm clad in the purest shimmering samite, held aloft Excalibur from the bosom of the water, signifying by divine providence that I, Arthur, was to carry Excalibur. THAT is why I am your king."

Dennis: [interrupting] "Listen, strange women lyin' in ponds distributin' swords is no basis for a system of government. Supreme executive power derives from a mandate from the masses, not from some farcical aquatic ceremony."

And of course although we know that handing out swords from a lake is not a basis for government, we do, for some bizarre reason, believe that people have somehow "learned" something just because we told them some facts five minutes ago. So what does an immediate test of a learner's "knowledge" **really** tell us? What can a learner **actually** recall a few hours, days or weeks after the training took place, and how much application to real-life performance do these tests really provide?

Before we answer these questions, let's go back to some facts. Nearly everything we know today about learning and forgetting was "discovered" by Hermann Ebbinghaus in the late 1800s. Ebbinghaus was a psychologist with a keen interest in memory and higher cognitive processes. He was the first to describe the "learning curve" and characterise the issues of memory retention. His experiments were clever; he systematically measured how long it took people to "memorise" new information and how much was retained over time by developing a series of nonsense syllables and words. During his experiments, subjects repeated a series of nonsense syllables and/or words as many times as was necessary to reach a competent level of accuracy (for example, three perfect reproductions without being prompted verbally or looking at it in writing). What he discovered was that the time required memorising nonsense syllables increased sharply as the number of syllables increased. I think we can all appreciate that it requires much more time and effort to memorise a 13-digit overseas telephone number than it does an eight-digit postcode.

Ebbinghaus also discovered that people are able to memorise more in distributed learning sessions (learning on more than one occasion) than by trying to assimilate everything in a single session. He then set out to determine the duration and strength of retention. Using a concept he invented called the "savings method" he determined the number of repetitions required to re-learn material and compared it to the number of repetitions initially required to learn the material. The more repetitions that were required, the more had been forgotten.

What he discovered through these experiments are things we intuitively know today. Firstly, items that are associated with one another are more easily remembered together. These associations could be due to congruity (e.g. they appeared next to each other on the list) or remote association (e.g. the learner made some connections between the two items in their own mind). Secondly, we remember best what we FIRST and LAST encounter (the so-called primacy/recency effect) and we tend to forget the middle items. Thirdly, even small amounts of practice, far less than what is required for mastery, leads to improved retention over time. Finally, most of us tend to forget about fifty percent of newly-learned knowledge in a matter of days or weeks. But the speed of forgetting is related to a number of factors. Most importantly, our ability to learn nonsense material (e.g. things we don't understand) is quite poor, requiring a great deal of effort, and the forgetting curve is quite steep. On the other hand, meaningful material (e.g. things that make sense because they relate to things we already know) takes only about one tenth of the effort to learn and the forgetting is relatively gradual. Not surprisingly, the forgetting curve is nearly flat for vivid or traumatic experiences, perhaps because the learner "revisits" the memory repetitively in his/her mind.

So, knowing all this research, why do we **still** feel that immediate "results" derived from post-course tests are the same as learning? As we know (and have seen above), after a few days, most of the "learning" has been lost. Perhaps we should challenge our learning providers that if we forget so much of what they supposedly teach us, we should get an appropriate discount on the price. Now **that** would be interesting!

It looks as though Kirkpatrick Level 2 doesn't fare that well either! Perhaps Level 3 will provide us with some concrete measures (at last). Let's take a look . . .

Kirkpatrick Level 3

This level of Kirkpatrick is all about behaviour, i.e. has the learning that has been "learned" actually been used back in the workplace in the form of changed behaviour. And this is where we start to get closer to really useful measures—but again it's still not that easy.

Although People Professionals can clearly set the foundations for behaviour change, all too often if the new behaviour can't be used or applied quickly enough in the workplace then it will inevitably be lost. Not only do new behaviours need to be used quickly, they also need to be used frequently so that they become habitual.

But if the new behaviours cannot be put into practice, they cannot become habits. And if they cannot become habits then surely most (if not all) of the money spent on the training is wasted! According to research on the formation of habits in a paper published in the *European Journal of Social Psychology*, Phillippa Lally and her colleagues from University College London looked at just how long it took to form a new habit. Phillippa found that many of the people in the study showed a curved relationship between practice and automaticity as shown below. Phillippa and her team found that, on average, it took 66 days for something to become as much of a habit as it would ever become.

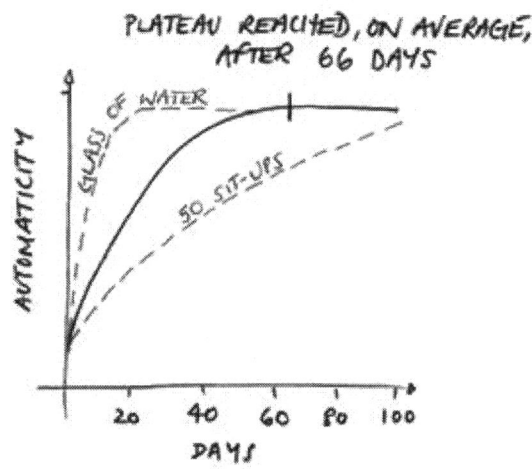

Although the average was 66 days, there was marked variation in how long habits took to form—anywhere from 18 days up to 254 days for the habits examined in this study. As you'd imagine, drinking a daily glass of water became automatic very quickly but doing 50 sit-ups before breakfast required more dedication (above, dotted lines).

So let's stand back for a moment and see what this research is telling us. On average it takes **66 days'** effort for something to become habitual. So unless when we've had our training course we use our new-found skills almost immediately, we'll forget most of what we've just learned and unless we practise our new-found skills solidly for about 66 days they won't become second nature to us. Doesn't paint a very good picture, does it? With this in mind, perhaps even Kirkpatrick Level 3 doesn't work in the way we thought it should, so let's see if Level 4 can finally deliver something we can use!

Kirkpatrick Level 4

So here we are at Level 4 of the Kirkpatrick model. This level is all about results and the effect that the people function is having on the business.

Although this is the most difficult level of evaluation, there are many people, including those senior managers and executives who've paid for everything in the first place, who want to know that their investment is having some form of positive impact. As we've seen from Levels 1, 2 and 3, most of the so-called "evaluation metrics" provide little, if anything, in the way of meaningful business results.

But again, let's step back for a moment. As People Professionals we know that we exist to serve our learners and ultimately our business and yet why do so many of us find it so hard to show benefit within our business? I'd like to suggest it's because many try and show value via the calculation of ROI (return on investment) rather than by other means. Let's look at this a bit further.

According to the book "Funky Business" by Kjell Nordstrom and Jonas Ridderstrale, Motorola calculates that every dollar invested in learning and development reaps $33 profit. That's fantastic, but wait a minute; **if** Motorola really did make $33 for every $1 invested in learning and development, then the best thing that they could possibly do would be to get out of electronics and move lock, stock and barrel into the learning! But of course, this is total nonsense; the $33 figure only works when looking at returns over the very long-term and of course you need to be an exceptionally successful company in the first place to drive this level of "return"!

The fight to prove the link between the people function and business success has brought us all sorts of wonderful metrics. According to the American Society for Training and Development, investment in employee training enhances a company's financial performance. An increase of $680 in a company's training expenditure per employee generates, on average, a six percent improvement in total shareholder return. Based on the training investments of 575 companies during a three-year period, researchers found that firms investing the most in training and development (measured by total investment per employee and percentage of total gross payroll) yielded a 36.9% total shareholder return as compared with a 25.5% weighted return for the Standard & Poors 500 index for the same period. That's a return 45% higher than the market average. These same firms also enjoyed higher profit margins and higher income per employee.

But wait a minute, aren't we in danger of revisiting the "training days per year" measure I spoke about in Part I? And anyway, what came first: the training or the successful organisation? You see (surprise, surprise), successful organisations **have** to spend more money on L&D to maintain their market position. Successful companies, especially those with exceptionally strong brands, have more to lose if their people are poorly trained. In short, they can't afford **not** to spend the money!

The return on your investment

OK, so we know that all sorts of claims are made about the organisational benefits of the people function, but why on earth should **you** do all this work to show the benefits? For most People Professionals the reasons are that it:

- measures the contribution of the people function,
- measures priorities for the business,
- focuses on results rather than inputs,
- alters perception of training, and
- alters perception of yourself!

But it's not always that easy, as we shall see. Calculating the ROI of your people activities is a complex and time-consuming process.

One of the leaders in this field is Jack Phillips, whose book "Return on Investment in Training and Performance Improvement Programs" is often seen as the "bible" for how to do ROI. In his book, Jack shows the following process for identifying the key components for the ROI calculation:

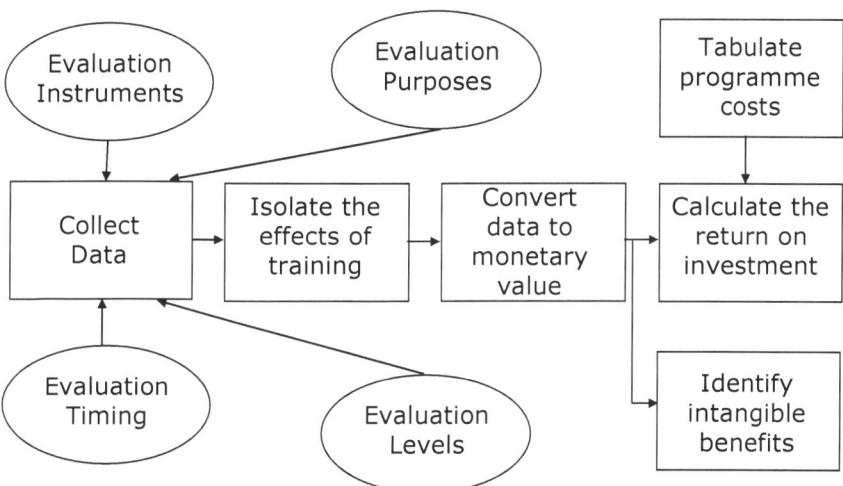

Although this is a time-consuming calculation (and one that many people find very difficult to do well), one of the key problems is the ability (or otherwise) to isolate the effects of the training from everything else that could be going on. Businesses are complex systems and only rarely will your interventions be the only input to raising performance; there are just so many other factors to take into account. Let's take a closer look at this.

Let's imagine that you've commissioned some personal development to increase the sales within your organisation. Six months after everyone has completed their training, sales have risen by ten percent. That's good, right? Well, maybe yes and maybe no. Rising sales are certainly what you're looking for, but was this as a direct result of the intervention, or were other issues affecting sales? For example:

- a major advertising campaign,
- a reduction in the selling price of your products against those of your competition,
- a major competitor exiting the market,
- the market as a whole increased by ten percent,

. . . or any number of literally hundreds of other possibilities!

To be brutally honest, although People Professionals will argue that the intervention was the thing that had the major effect on sales, as you can see it's all too easy for other elements of the business to prove otherwise.

There are other issues too. ROI is a historical measure—it measures what's happened and therefore it's possible for you to discover that you've already invested unwisely and that unfortunately you can't "undo" your investment. There's also the assumption (often made by the business itself) that the greater the investment, the greater the returns, which isn't always the case! Added to that, there are no generally accepted benchmarks for ROI. Take a moment to think about what **is** a good ROI? Many websites tell you **how** to calculate ROI, though none I can find really tell you **what** an ideal ROI is. And there's a really good reason for this—there isn't an ideal ROI for training! That's right; there isn't an ideal ROI for training in general, or indeed for any training programme specifically.

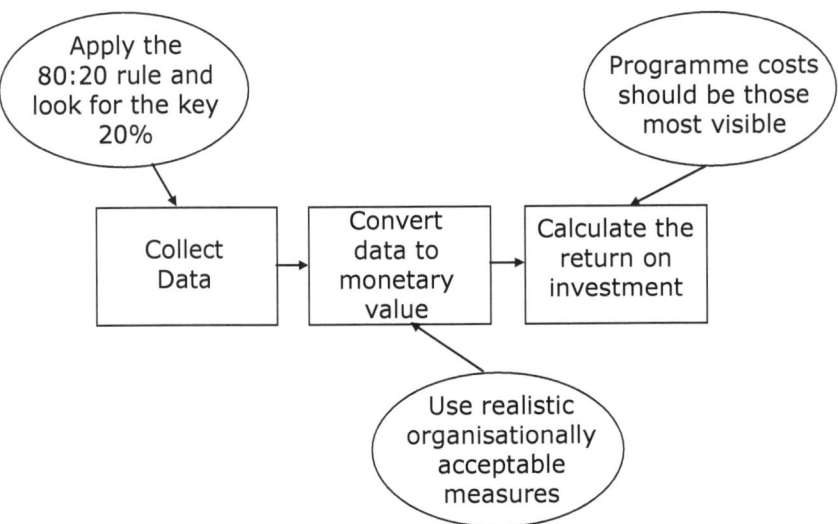

Yet although ROI has no "definite value" for the people function there is, however, an almost insatiable appetite for it to be calculated. Forum upon forum has people asking how best to calculate this "magical" figure, what the issues are with getting it right and so on. If you **really** want to calculate ROI (and because the isolation of external events is just so difficult and contentious) you may want to look at the above model that I've developed. This is an amended version of the Jack Phillips model; it's not perfect, but it will make your task easier.

Here are some other "issues" with ROI that you may also want to consider:

- you can't provide an ROI for everything—much as you may want to!
- ROI is **not** the same as BCR (benefit cost ratio)—although many people confuse these.
- Saving money through any learning project is not the same as ROI—it's just saving money! Yet again, many people also confuse these.
- Project comparisons are **not** the same as ROI.

So, as you can see, there are many issues with calculating ROI, but by far the biggest issue is what any answer **actually** means. Care should always be taken here; a low ROI may achieve financial results no better than putting your money in a standard deposit account, whereas a very high ROI might be seen as being a manipulated result by your senior business managers. Perhaps something more suitable is required?

Sometimes even doing nothing gets results!

It's a strange but true phenomenon that there are times when doing nothing (or very little) will actually deliver positive results! Here are a couple of examples:

Firstly, your best people will almost certainly deliver your best results. I recall reading an article about an organisation that **only** invested in the best sales people because they would **always** outperform the rest of the pack. You see, in almost every form of business, your best people will always yield your best results.

Secondly, just watching people can yield amazing results (not literally watching them, but making sure they know their performance is being monitored). The now famous 'Hawthorne effect' showed that people increase their productivity when they know they're being observed.

Think about this; no real investment, no training but still an increase in performance. Nirvana surely, but of course it's not in any way sustainable over the long-term.

Return on Expectations (ROE)

Returning to Kirkpatrick for one last time, more recent developments in the evaluation model now point to the belief that "The End" is "The Beginning". What is meant here is that before a training programme is designed and delivered there's a need to find out what results are expected. In simple terms, you need a need to find out what success will "look like" for your business leaders so you can better focus your training in order to meet those expectations. I don't mean to be overly blunt here, but who on earth would ever contemplate designing a training course **without** knowing what a good result looks like! I mean, Jeez; isn't this what a good training needs analysis (TNA) should do anyway?

As with the other Levels of Kirkpatrick, much has been written about ROE. One example is the words from the Kirkpatrick people themselves, who say:

> "The great thing about ROE is that the stakeholder is in control of determining what is important to them and you, as a training professional, have the ability to determine with their agreement the best ways to measure the results."

Perhaps I'm losing the plot here, but surely the stakeholder (that's the business) should **always** be in control of the training they need! What we need is something far simpler for everyone and I may just have the answer . . .

The love making approach

We're nearing the end of this article and when combined with Part I, we've covered a great deal of ground. But despite all the measures and techniques I've explored in these two articles, I believe that in business so much comes back to what I rather cheekily refer to as "The love making approach". You know the one; you've just finished making love with your partner and one of you mutters those immortal words, "Darling, how was it for you?" That's right—simple and to the point. After all, (hopefully) when you've made love, you don't get out a four-point Likert scale to assess the food, ambiance or pre-course reading!

Now you may think I've gone a little mad here, but bear with me. All too often we try and manipulate the benefit of L&D within the organisation; we try and put numbers to things that are notoriously difficult to measure and we try and sell success to our managers when often there is little more than a tenuous link. Of course, if you can clearly measure benefits that the people function has delivered, then do so, but bear in mind that asking the "How was it for you?" question can sometimes be far more powerful.

Asking senior managers this question immediately involves them in the results. Why should you have to tell them how your L&D has made their lives easier? If they can't see it for themselves then it could be argued it hasn't worked! When you get the reply listen and act upon it. Rarely is anything perfect the first time and with the people function it can be a lifetime's work to achieve deep changes within a business, so learn from what you've done, improve it and move on.

For those of you who think this is little more than the Level 1 questions I belittled earlier, think again. Remember, you're **not** asking the learner, you're asking the business—and if the business is happy that the results were what they wanted, job done!

Conclusions

This chapter has provided you with quite a journey. We've looked at common problems with trying to measure people moments, we've explored some of the science behind KPIs and I've put forward some clear arguments that Kirkpatrick may not (after all) be the best way to evaluate your learning and development. This journey is never complete. Hopefully you've gained further insights into the world of measuring L&D and will gain even more insights as you put many of the techniques explored here into practice.

Chapter 11: Activities

There's been a great deal to take on board in this chapter. By way of consolidating the learning, I'd suggest you try the following activities.

1. Take a fresh look at your current people measures and reflect on their effectiveness.

2. For each of the headings "input", "process" and "output", consider what would best make a suite of measures for your business.

3. For each of the measures identified above, construct a number of KPIs so that you can easily track progress.

4. Identify which KPIs could lead to perverse consequences and ensure that you've some "wobble board" measures in place to track these.

5. Identify what good business performance looks like in your business.

12

Measuring Alignment

"Great things are not done by impulse, but by a series of things brought together."

Vincent Van Gogh
Dutch post-Impressionist painter whose work, notable for its rough beauty, emotional honesty and bold colour, had a far-reaching influence on 20th-century art.

Introduction

This book has provided a wealth of information, ideas and suggestions that will enable you to become aligned with your business, reaping the rewards as a result. In this chapter we'll take a look at how you can actually measure alignment within your business. As with all things people-related, measurement isn't an exact science, but it will provide a highly indicative position of where you are on your journey and give you areas for focus and improvement.

Measuring organisational alignment

According to the *Aligning learning to strategic priorities* discussion paper from the Chartered Institute of Personnel and Development (CIPD):

> "Alignment is clearly a good thing to aspire to, but achieving it in practice is difficult. One challenge is maintaining alignment in the dynamic and fast-moving environment in which many organisations operate. Organisational priorities can change and develop, sometimes with alarming rapidity."

If the CIPD thinks that achieving alignment is difficult, then measuring alignment also becomes a difficult activity, but one that's possible to do. In this book I've covered a wide range of issues that, as People Professionals, you'll need to focus on in order to achieve alignment.

Measuring each of the individual aspects of alignment isn't easy. Measuring strategy and value propositions and culture and structure and execution and talent and mergers etc. would not only create a questionnaire as long as your arm, it would also be rather cumbersome to administer. There is, however, a way of grouping the key aspects of alignment into three high-level categories which makes the process of measuring alignment so much easier. The three high-level categories are:

1. Clarity—do people know what's important within the business?
2. Consistency—are planned activities consistent with what's important?
3. Commitment—does the business follow through by allocating resources?

Let's look at each of these in turn.

1. Clarity

Clarity is the bedrock of alignment. Without clarity it's impossible to be aligned. In chapter 1 I talked about the importance of seeing eye-to-eye with your business and as People Professionals, this means two key things:

I. knowing and understanding the plans and priorities of the business, and
II. ensuring the business knows and understands how the people function is supporting these plans and priorities.

As People Professionals you absolutely, without question, must **thoroughly** understand the plans and priorities of your business. This means far more than just taking a cursory glance through any strategy document that happens to be lying around; rather it's a deep and questioning approach to what your business is focusing on, the direction in which it's heading and the challenges it's facing.

As People Professionals you must **totally** understand the issues your business is facing because if you don't you can't begin to address them. You need to understand thoroughly the strategy of your business and understand how that applies to and impacts on **you.** Clarity of the business strategy is essential, because without that you'll never achieve alignment. This was highlighted in a Chartered Institute of Personnel and Development (CIPD) online poll conducted in November 2007, where 46% of respondents said that, in their organisation, the overall strategy was unclear and therefore difficult to align against.

Once you have a thorough understanding of the business strategy you'll naturally need to develop a response in support of it. In chapter 6 we looked at how to develop a great strategy and within your strategy you'll naturally need to consider how to develop and deliver appropriate interventions that support it. Unfortunately, this is where things can become unstuck. People Professionals need to develop interventions and solutions that the business **believes** will have an impact. If not, then the business will look upon the people function as being "out of step" with the business and therefore not aligned.

I've seen just about every fad imaginable aimed at making people better at what they do. Some of these have been based on scientific research such as psychometric tools and some have been much more "fun-based", such as drumming workshops. Regardless of the interventions you select, your business must completely understand the **reason** why these interventions were selected and the benefits they will bring. All too often I've seen interventions fail because People Professionals hadn't spent enough time engaging with the business and explaining why they were adopting various approaches and the benefits they would bring.

Stop right now!

Go back a few paragraphs to when I talked about the CIPD online poll. If for any reason you're not totally clear about the strategy, strategic direction, goals or aims of your organisation then go and find out. Do not under any circumstances attempt to move forward until you thoroughly understand the following:

- the vision of the organisation,
- its goals or aims for this year and the next three to five years,
- operational challenges e.g. cost pressures, new plant and machinery, mergers, acquisitions, new markets etc.,
- pressures from competitors,
- value proposition of the organisation or its products, and
- high-level financial information such as income, expenditure, margins etc.

Clarity needs to occur at all levels within a business. In my experience, the further you travel away from senior management, both in terms of status and physical distance, the less clarity there tends to be. I'm sure that most of you reading this book will at some point have played the game "Chinese Whispers" where the message is altered slightly from person to person until the final message bears little, if any, similarity to the starting message. A classic example of this is the old army message of "Send reinforcements, we're going to advance" which, by the time it's travelled to its intended recipients, has become "Send three and fourpence, we're going to a dance". Distance and changes in status are major causes of key messages becoming distorted and are two of the reasons why large organisations invest so heavily in internal communication teams—because they need to ensure that the right messages are reinforced in the right way, always.

The story is told of how President John Kennedy once visited NASA. He came across a cleaner and asked him what his job was. The cleaner replied: "My job is to help to put a man on the moon." There's always been a discussion of whether this story is true or not, but what it illustrates is the cleaner's complete alignment with the aims of NASA, its collective mission and strategy. This was clearly a great eye-to-eye moment.

2. Consistency

Consistency is about ensuring that all planned activities and interventions that will be delivered via the people function are consistent with what's important for the business. Let's look at this in a little more detail.

Let's suppose that the strategy process has identified that a business needs to:

- drive sales for all consumer products,
- reduce operating costs for contact centres,
- recruit a hundred high-calibre engineering graduates.

The business would naturally expect the people function to be involved in responding to the above in an appropriate manner. Some of the planned interventions may include:

- additional sales training for all staff working with consumer products,
- analysis of contact centres to identify opportunities for rationalisation, which mayinclude changes to processes or increased training for staff, and
- partnering with appropriate universities to secure early identification of suitable graduates.

There would be many more interventions you could develop to address the issues above, but I'm sure you get the picture. As long as the proposed interventions are seen to be consistent with the needs of the business, then all's well.

However, the people function may have decided to develop interventions such as:

- outward bound courses,
- drumming workshops,
- team building workshops for contact centre staff,
- social media recruitment for arts and humanities graduates,

- disciplinary action for consumer product sales people who miss their targets.

If the above interventions are put to the business it will rightly think that the people function does not fully understand the key issues and is proposing to deliver interventions that are inconsistent with its focus and direction. Remember, if a business sees its people function operating in a manner that is inconsistent with the overall goals of the business, it will think they are misaligned. It is therefore critical that all activities, interventions and effort is consistent with the needs of the business. Anything else is a failure.

3. Commitment

Commitment is about both the business and People Professionals committing to the promises they've made. This relies on two key items:

I. the business "putting its money where its mouth is" and providing adequate funding and resources for agreed interventions, and
II. the people function executing and delivering the interventions as planned.

A business will only "put its money where its mouth is" if the people function has clearly demonstrated both clarity and consistency. Today, many People Professionals are facing the challenges of funding, budgets and outsourcing. As we've seen throughout this book, funding and budgets will always be a challenge for People Professionals, but even more so if they are unable to demonstrate clarity and consistency because a business will **only** commit resources if it believes its money will be used to the best effect. Where a business is unconvinced of the benefits of interventions, it is less likely to invest, and where it remains unconvinced of the overall value of an intervention or of any aspect of the people function, it will either choose not to fund it, or will tend to outsource it.

Although a business may provide the resources and funding for specific interventions the people function still needs to ensure these interventions are executed and delivered as required by the business. Providing a new product course two weeks after the product has launched isn't going to win you any favours and definitely isn't a sign of commitment. As we saw in earlier chapters, the need to execute and deliver is critical to success and is proof that you are delivering on your promises. Gaining commitment from your business is therefore the key goal for the People Professional. Without commitment from the business nothing will be delivered.

Measuring alignment with your business

Having outlined that alignment can be measured through clarity, consistency and commitment, let's look at how you actually go about doing this.

Measuring the level of alignment within your business can be carried out in a number of ways. For optimum results I'd suggest using an online survey. This will give you reach across a business and will also provide you with speed and simplicity. To help you get started, I've provided some initial questions in Appendix D, which you can use to construct a series of tailored statements which can then be assessed via a five-point Likert scale, where five is "strongly agree" and one is "strongly disagree". I've also provided an example survey which you can tailor for your own use.

There are a number of excellent, readily available online survey packages and many businesses already have licences for one or more of these. Even if your business doesn't currently have a licence, these can normally be purchased for a very reasonable amount.

Measuring clarity

When measuring clarity it's critical to know the extent by which the people function understands the strategy, plans and priorities for the business and it's equally critical for the business to recognise the solutions offered by the people function.

This seeing eye-to-eye is the foundation of clarity and without clarity there can never be any alignment.

When measuring clarity, some of the questions you may want to consider are:

Clarity of the business plans:

- Does the people function know the strategy, plans and priorities of the business?
- Are these plans known by everyone, or just the senior management?
- Can the people function articulate, in simple terms, what they are going to do for the business to support the strategy?
- Does the people function feel that its plans for the business are credible and realistic?
- Does the people function believe that its planned interventions are aligned with the overall business plan?

Clarity of the people function plans:

- Does the business know the strategy, plans and priorities of the people function?
- Are these plans known by everyone, or just the senior management?
- Can people across the business articulate, in simple terms, what the people function is going to do for them or their business unit?
- Do people across the business feel that the plans being offered by the people function are credible and realistic?
- Do people across the business feel that the planned interventions from the people function are aligned with the overall business plan?

Measuring consistency

Measuring consistency is about assessing whether planned activities to be delivered by the people function are consistent with what's important for the business. Remember, if the business does not see that planned interventions are consistent with its strategy, there cannot be alignment.

When measuring consistency, some of the questions you may want to consider are:

- Does the people function develop interventions that are consistent with the needs of the business?
- Does the business believe that the interventions developed by the people function are consistent with the needs of the business?
- Does the business believe that interventions developed by the people function are consistent with its values?
- Does the people function take a long-term view of people and business issues and keep working at ideas until they are resolved?
- Does the people function ensure that short-term issues do not detract from long-term business goals?
- Do the activities planned by the people function at each location and for each individual align with the overall business plan?
- Are executives, senior managers, managers and staff confident that planned people-based activities can be delivered?
- Are executives, senior managers, managers and staff aware of the difference between cost and value where people initiatives are concerned?

Measuring commitment

The final measure we're looking at is commitment. This is a measure of the business's desire to commit resources and follow through to deliver on the areas it deems important. Essentially, does the business "put its money where its mouth is"? When measuring commitment we also need to consider the commitment of the people function, i.e. is it committed to delivering on the promises it's made to the business?

When measuring commitment, some of the questions you may want to consider are:

- Does the business "put its money where its mouth is"—does it follow through on its promises?
- Does the people function organise itself to ensure that interventions are delivered to the timescales required by the business?
- Do executives, senior managers, managers and staff measure their ability to deliver on people issues within the business plan before making promises?
- Do executives, senior managers, managers and staff allocate the correct amount of resources to ensure people initiatives are implemented as planned?
- Within the business, is there a strong feeling that people priorities set out in the business plan will be delivered on time **and** budget?
- Within the business, if people issues are important, will they be resourced and managed correctly?
- Does the people function use metrics to help predict future performance rather than just measure current or past performance?

Pulling it all together

Having looked at the questions above, it's now time to start pulling your own survey together. When doing this, take time to consider the target audience and make sure that the questions are phrased correctly. I once made the mistake of sending out the following question:

"At my location, we all know what the business goals are."

Unfortunately I hadn't taken enough account of the target audience, who were all either engineers or scientists. Asking this group to confirm that "we all know" turned out to be the wrong thing to do. Comments were received along the lines of "How can I possibly know if everyone knows what the business goals are?" or "I can only confirm my own views" or "I cannot speak for others". I'd forgotten that engineers and scientists are exceptionally precise people and I should have been more precise in the way I phrased my question.

When you've settled on your questions you can format your final questionnaire using your preferred online survey tool and once you've received the responses then it's time to analyse the results.

Each of the online survey tools has its own set of analysis tools. Some of these are comprehensive, whereas others can be rather rudimentary. One of the best approaches that I've found is to download all the results into a spreadsheet and then use pivot tables to analyse the results rapidly, using the built-in graph function.

What does good look like?

Whenever you measure something there's always pressure from senior management to compare your results against those from other businesses or for you to demonstrate that the results you've got somehow show that you're doing well compared with some well-known norms. When you're measuring alignment please be aware that it's not possible to compare your results with those from other businesses. The results that you get are the results within **your** business. They cannot be directly compared with other businesses or against measured norms. The results you get will simply show how aligned **your** business is. To be frank, it doesn't matter how aligned any other business is; what matters most is how aligned (or otherwise) **your** business is. Nothing else matters.

One of the techniques I've used to demonstrate the level of alignment within a business is to apply a weighting to each question. Some online survey tools will do this for you, but if not then it's a fairly simple thing to do once you've downloaded your results into a spreadsheet. Take a look at the example below:

Q #	Statement	Strongly agree	Agree	Don't know	Disagree	Strongly disagree
1	I know and understand the current business goals					
Weight		+2	+1	0	-1	-2

In this example I'll give +2 points for each time a respondent answers "strongly agree", +1 point for every "agree", zero points for a "don't know",—1 point for "disagree" and—2 points for a "strongly disagree". By using this approach it's possible to weight the overall responses and demonstrate how positive, neutral or negative the alignment is for each question asked. Combining all the scores for each of the categories (clarity, consistency and commitment) will also give you an indication of alignment at a higher level. Let's work through an example.

Let's assume that you've surveyed a hundred people. If we focus on question one (above), let's assume that of the 100 responses:

- 30 were "strongly agree"
- 40 were "agree"
- 20 were "don't know"
- 5 were "disagree" and
- 5 were "strongly disagree"

Applying the weighting (shown above) we would then have:

30 x +2 = +60

40 x +1 = +40

20 x 0 = 0

5 x -1 = -5

5 x -2 = -10

Adding the above up we get a total of 85 (60+40+0+(-5)+(-10)). The maximum score that could have been gained from 100 people would of course have been 200 (100 x +2). So, as a percentage, 85/200 is 42.5%. As 50% represents the overall neutral score, we can now say that, given the above responses, the actual alignment is 7.5% negative (42.5-50). In this case there's no positive alignment score and therefore these responses would represent something of a problem to a business, i.e. that at the most basic level people did not have a positive idea of what the current business goals were.

But let's suppose that the responses had been somewhat different with:

- 60 saying "strongly agree"
- 20 saying "agree"
- 10 saying "don't know"
- 5 saying "disagree" and
- 5 saying "strongly disagree"

Applying the weightings (just as before) we would now have:

60 x +2 = +120

20 x +1 = +20

10 x 0 = 0

5 x -1 = -5

5 x -2 = -10

Adding the above up we get a total of 125 (120+20+0+(-5)+(-10)). As before, the maximum score that could have been gained would have been 200 (100 x +2). So, as a percentage, 125/200 is 62.5%. As 50% represents the overall neutral score, we can now say that, given the above responses, the actual alignment is 12.5% positive. This means that overall the survey respondents have a positive view of the current business goals.

Conclusions

Measuring alignment is not only possible within your business, it's absolutely essential. As you've seen in this chapter, alignment can be measured quite simply by using commonly available online tools. By grouping survey questions into the categories of clarity, consistency and commitment it's possible to understand the level of alignment within your business and spot any areas for improvement.

Measuring alignment allows you to understand and address issues within your business: issues which could be preventing you from achieving success or accessing much-needed resources. Take time to measure alignment within your business. You may be surprised by what you find!

Chapter 12: Activities

For this chapter, I suggest you use the sample survey in Appendix D or devise your own survey and begin to measure alignment within your business. It's important for you to realise that you don't need to measure everything at once. You can start by measuring the amount of clarity within your business and then, depending on the results, you can either remedy negative views or move forward and commence the measurement of consistency and commitment. Take small but measured (no pun intended) steps along the following lines:

- Start by measuring clarity within your business. If you get a neutral or negative score then increase the level of stakeholder communications and measure the clarity scores again in three to six months' time.
- If the overall score for clarity is positive, check the scores for each of the questions to see if there are any specific areas of weakness that may need further attention.
- When you have a positive score for clarity, widen your survey to include the consistency questions. As before, check that the overall score is positive.
- If the overall score for consistency is positive, check the scores for each of the questions to see if there are any specific areas of weakness that may need further attention. Then widen your survey to include the final set of questions relating to commitment.
- If the overall score for consistency is negative, check that your planned interventions are aligned with business needs. Adjust as necessary.
- If the overall score for commitment is positive then, as before, check the scores for each of the questions to see if there are any specific areas of weakness that may need further attention. As a rule of thumb, if you have a positive commitment score then you're on your way to being truly aligned. Well done!
- If the overall score for commitment is negative, check to ensure that the business is "putting its money where its mouth is" and that the people function is actually delivering on its promises. Adjust as necessary.

APPENDIX A

Nokia's Burning Platform

Introduction

Here's the full text of Nokia CEO Stephen Elop's "Burning Platform" memo, which outlines missed opportunities and identifies multiple strategic challenges to the mobile phone company.

It was reported on the 9th February, 2011 ahead of a Nokia analyst briefing in London, in which Mr. Elop was expected to announce big changes to the company's strategy and senior management.

This was an exceptionally bold move. Only time will tell if it is right, or enough.

Full text of the memo

"Hello there.

There is a pertinent story about a man who was working on an oil platform in the North Sea. He woke up one night from a loud explosion, which suddenly set his entire oil platform on fire. In mere moments, he was surrounded by flames. Through the smoke and heat, he barely made his way out of the chaos to the platform's edge. When he looked down over the edge, all he could see were the dark, cold, foreboding Atlantic waters.

As the fire approached him, the man had mere seconds to react. He could stand on the platform, and inevitably be consumed by the burning flames. Or, he could plunge 30 meters in to the freezing waters. The man was standing upon a "burning platform," and he needed to make a choice.

He decided to jump. It was unexpected. In ordinary circumstances, the man would never consider plunging into icy waters. But these were not ordinary times—his platform was on fire. The man survived the fall and the waters. After he was rescued, he noted that a "burning platform" caused a radical change in his behaviour.

We too, are standing on a "burning platform," and we must decide how we are going to change our behaviour.

Over the past few months, I've shared with you what I've heard from our shareholders, operators, developers, suppliers and from you. Today, I'm going to share what I've learned and what I have come to believe.

I have learned that we are standing on a burning platform.

And, we have more than one explosion—we have multiple points of scorching heat that are fuelling a blazing fire around us.

For example, there is intense heat coming from our competitors, more rapidly than we ever expected. Apple disrupted the market by redefining the smartphone and attracting developers to a closed, but very powerful ecosystem.

In 2008, Apple's market share in the $300+ price range was 25 percent; by 2010 it escalated to 61 percent. They are enjoying a tremendous growth trajectory with a 78 percent earnings growth year over year in Q4 2010. Apple demonstrated that if designed well, consumers would buy a high-priced phone with a great experience and developers would build applications. They changed the game, and today, Apple owns the high-end range.

And then, there is Android. In about two years, Android created a platform that attracts application developers, service providers and hardware manufacturers. Android came in at the high-end, they are now winning the mid-range, and quickly they are going downstream to phones under €100. Google has become a gravitational force, drawing much of the industry's innovation to its core.

Let's not forget about the low-end price range. In 2008, MediaTek supplied complete reference designs for phone chipsets, which enabled manufacturers in the Shenzhen region of China to produce phones at an unbelievable pace. By some accounts, this ecosystem now produces more than one third of the phones sold globally—taking share from us in emerging markets.

While competitors poured flames on our market share, what happened at Nokia? We fell behind, we missed big trends, and we lost time. At that time, we thought we were making the right decisions; but, with the benefit of hindsight, we now find ourselves years behind.

The first iPhone shipped in 2007, and we still don't have a product that is close to their experience. Android came on the scene just over 2 years ago, and this week they took our leadership position in smartphone volumes. Unbelievable.

We have some brilliant sources of innovation inside Nokia, but we are not bringing it to market fast enough. We thought MeeGo would be a platform for winning high-end smartphones. However, at this rate, by the end of 2011, we might have only one MeeGo product in the market.

At the midrange, we have Symbian. It has proven to be non-competitive in leading markets like North America. Additionally, Symbian is proving to be an increasingly difficult environment in which to develop to meet the continuously expanding consumer requirements, leading to slowness in product development and also creating a disadvantage when we seek to take advantage of new hardware platforms. As a result, if we continue like before, we will get further and further behind, while our competitors advance further and further ahead.

At the lower-end price range, Chinese OEMs are cranking out a device much faster than, as one Nokia employee said only partially in jest, "the time that it takes us to polish a PowerPoint presentation." They are fast, they are cheap, and they are challenging us.

And the truly perplexing aspect is that we're not even fighting with the right weapons. We are still too often trying to approach each price range on a device-to-device basis.

The battle of devices has now become a war of ecosystems, where ecosystems include not only the hardware and software of the device, but developers, applications, ecommerce, advertising, search, social applications, location-based services, unified communications and many other things. Our competitors aren't taking our market share with devices; they are taking our market share with an entire ecosystem. This means we're going to have to decide how we either build, catalyse or join an ecosystem.
This is one of the decisions we need to make. In the meantime, we've lost market share, we've lost mind share and we've lost time.

On Tuesday, Standard & Poor's informed that they will put our A long term and A-1 short term ratings on negative credit watch. This is a similar rating action to the one that Moody's took last week. Basically it means that during the next few weeks they will make an analysis of Nokia, and decide on a possible credit rating downgrade.

Why are these credit agencies contemplating these changes? Because they are concerned about our competitiveness.

Consumer preference for Nokia declined worldwide. In the UK, our brand preference has slipped to 20 percent, which is 8 percent lower than last year. That means only 1 out of 5 people in the UK prefer Nokia to other brands. It's also down in the other markets, which are traditionally our strongholds: Russia, Germany, Indonesia, UAE, and on and on and on.

How did we get to this point? Why did we fall behind when the world around us evolved?

This is what I have been trying to understand. I believe at least some of it has been due to our attitude inside Nokia. We poured gasoline on our own burning platform. I believe we have lacked accountability and leadership to align and direct the company through these disruptive times. We had a series of misses. We haven't been delivering innovation fast enough. We're not collaborating internally.

Nokia, our platform is burning.

We are working on a path forward—a path to rebuild our market leadership. When we share the new strategy on February 11, it will be a huge effort to transform our company. But, I believe that together, we can face the challenges ahead of us.

Together, we can choose to define our future.

The burning platform, upon which the man found himself, caused the man to shift his behaviour, and take a bold and brave step into an uncertain future. He was able to tell his story. Now, we have a great opportunity to do the same.

Stephen.

APPENDIX B

Amazon's Letter To Shareholders

Full text of the letter

1997 LETTER TO SHAREHOLDERS

(Reprinted from the 1997 Annual Report)

To our shareholders:

Amazon.com passed many milestones in 1997: by year-end, we had served more than 1.5 million customers, yielding 838% revenue growth to $147.8 million, and extended our market leadership despite aggressive ccompetitive entry.

But this is Day 1 for the Internet and, if we execute well, for Amazon.com. Today, online commerce saves customers money and precious time. Tomorrow, through personalization, online commerce will accelerate the very process of discovery. Amazon.com uses the Internet to create real value for its customers and, by doing so, hopes to create an enduring franchise, even in established and large markets.

We have a window of opportunity as larger players marshal the resources to pursue the online opportunity and as customers, new to purchasing online, are receptive to forming new relationships. The competitive landscape has continued to evolve at a fast pace. Many large players have moved online with credible offerings and have devoted substantial energy and resources to building awareness, traffic, and sales.

Our goal is to move quickly to solidify and extend our current position while we begin to pursue the online commerce opportunities in other areas. We see substantial opportunity in the large markets we are targeting. This strategy is not without risk: it requires serious investment and crisp execution against established franchise leaders.

It's All About the Long Term

We believe that a fundamental measure of our success will be the shareholder value we create over the long term. This value will be a direct result of our ability to extend and solidify our current market leadership position.

The stronger our market leadership, the more powerful our economic model. Market leadership can translate directly to higher revenue, higher profitability, greater capital velocity, and correspondingly stronger returns on invested capital.

Our decisions have consistently reflected this focus. We first measure ourselves in terms of the metrics most indicative of our market leadership: customer and revenue growth, the degree to which our customers continue to purchase from us on a repeat basis, and the strength of our brand. We have invested and will continue to invest aggressively to expand and leverage our customer base, brand, and infrastructure as we move to establish an enduring franchise.

Because of our emphasis on the long term, we may make decisions and weigh tradeoffs differently than
 some companies. Accordingly, we want to share with you our fundamental management and decision-making approach so that you, our shareholders, may confirm that it is consistent with your investment philosophy:

- We will continue to focus relentlessly on our customers.

- We will continue to make investment decisions in light of long-term market leadership considerations rather than short-term profitability considerations or short-term Wall Street reactions.

- We will continue to measure our programs and the effectiveness of our investments analytically, to jettison those that do not provide acceptable returns, and to step up our investment in those that work best. We will continue to learn from both our successes and our failures.• We will make bold rather than timid investment decisions where we see a sufficient probability of gaining market leadership advantages. Some of these investments will pay off, others will not, and we will have learned another valuable lesson in either case.

- When forced to choose between optimizing the appearance of our GAAP accounting and maximizing the present value of future cash flows, we'll take the cash flows.

- We will share our strategic thought processes with you when we make bold choices (to the extent competitive pressures allow), so that you may evaluate for yourselves whether we are making rational long-term leadership investments.

- We will work hard to spend wisely and maintain our lean culture. We understand the importance of continually reinforcing a cost-conscious culture, particularly in a business incurring net losses.

- We will balance our focus on growth with emphasis on long-term profitability and capital management.

At this stage, we choose to prioritize growth because we believe that scale is central to achieving the potential of our business model.

- We will continue to focus on hiring and retaining versatile and talented employees, and continue to weight their compensation to stock options rather than cash. We know our success will be largely affected by our ability to attract and retain a motivated employee base, each of whom must think like, and therefore must actually be, an owner.

We aren't so bold as to claim that the above is the "right" investment philosophy, but it's ours, and we would be remiss if we weren't clear in the approach we have taken and will continue to take. With this foundation, we would like to turn to a review of our business focus, our progress in 1997, and our outlook for the future.

Obsess Over Customers

From the beginning, our focus has been on offering our customers compelling value. We realized that the Web was, and still is, the World Wide Wait. Therefore, we set out to offer customers something they simply could not get any other way, and began serving them with books. We brought them much more selection than was possible in a physical store (our store would now occupy 6 football fields), and presented it in a useful, easyto-search, and easy-to-browse format in a store open 365 days a year, 24 hours a day. We maintained a dogged focus on improving the shopping experience, and in 1997 substantially enhanced our store. We now offer customers gift certificates, 1-ClickSM shopping, and vastly more reviews, content, browsing options, and recommendation features. We dramatically lowered prices, further increasing customer value. Word of mouth remains the most powerful customer acquisition tool we have, and we are grateful for the trust our customers have placed in us. Repeat purchases and word of mouth have combined to make Amazon.com the market leader in online bookselling.

By many measures, Amazon.com came a long way in 1997:

- Sales grew from $15.7 million in 1996 to $147.8 million—an 838% increase.

- Cumulative customer accounts grew from 180,000 to 1,510,000—a 738% increase.

- The percentage of orders from repeat customers grew from over 46% in the fourth quarter of 1996 to over 58% in the same period in 1997.

- In terms of audience reach, per Media Metrix, our Web site went from a rank of 90th to within the top 20.

- We established long-term relationships with many important strategic partners, including America Online, Yahoo!, Excite, Netscape, GeoCities, AltaVista, @Home, and Prodigy.

Infrastructure

During 1997, we worked hard to expand our business infrastructure to support these greatly increased traffic, sales, and service levels:

- Amazon.com's employee base grew from 158 to 614, and we significantly strengthened our management team.

- Distribution center capacity grew from 50,000 to 285,000 square feet, including a 70% expansion of our Seattle facilities and the launch of our second distribution center in Delaware in November.

- Inventories rose to over 200,000 titles at year-end, enabling us to improve availability for our customers.

- Our cash and investment balances at year-end were $125 million, thanks to our initial public offering in May 1997 and our $75 million loan, affording us substantial strategic flexibility.

Our Employees

The past year's success is the product of a talented, smart, hard-working group, and I take great pride in being a part of this team. Setting the bar high in our approach to hiring has been, and will continue to be, the single most important element of Amazon.com's success.

It's not easy to work here (when I interview people I tell them, "You can work long, hard, or smart, but at Amazon.com you can't choose two out of three"), but we are working to build something important, something that matters to our customers, something that we can all tell our grandchildren about. Such things aren't meant to be easy. We are incredibly fortunate to have this group of dedicated employees whose sacrifices and passion build Amazon.com.

Goals for 1998

We are still in the early stages of learning how to bring new value to our customers through Internet commerce and merchandising. Our goal remains to continue to solidify and extend our brand and customer base. This requires sustained investment in systems and infrastructure to support outstanding customer convenience, selection, and service while we grow. We are planning to add music to our product offering, and over time we believe that other products may be prudent investments. We also believe there are significant opportunities to better serve our customers overseas, such as reducing delivery times and better tailoring the customer experience.

To be certain, a big part of the challenge for us will lie not in finding new ways to expand our business, but in prioritizing our investments.

We now know vastly more about online commerce than when Amazon.com was founded, but we still have so much to learn. Though we are optimistic, we must remain vigilant and maintain a sense of urgency. The challenges and hurdles we will face to make our long-term vision for Amazon.com a reality are several: aggressive, capable, well-funded competition; considerable growth challenges and execution risk; the risks of product and geographic expansion; and the need for large continuing investments to meet an expanding market opportunity. However, as we've long said, online bookselling, and online commerce in general, should prove to be a very large market, and it's likely that a number of companies will see significant benefit. We feel good about what we've done, and even more excited about what we want to do.

1997 was indeed an incredible year. We at Amazon.com are grateful to our customers for their business and trust, to each other for our hard work, and to our shareholders for their support and encouragement.

Jeffrey P. Bezos

Founder and Chief Executive Officer

Amazon.com, Inc.

APPENDIX C

Johnson & Johnson Credo

Our Credo

We believe our first responsibility is to the doctors, nurses and patients, to mothers and fathers and all others who use our products and services.

In meeting their needs everything we do must be of high quality.

We must constantly strive to reduce our costs in order to maintain reasonable prices.

Customers' orders must be serviced promptly and accurately. Our suppliers and distributors must have an opportunity to make a fair profit.

We are responsible to our employees, the men and women who work with us throughout the world. Everyone must be considered as an individual.

We must respect their dignity and recognize their merit. They must have a sense of security in their jobs. Compensation must be fair and adequate, and working conditions clean, orderly and safe. We must be mindful of ways to help our employees fulfil their family responsibilities. Employees must feel free to make suggestions and complaints. There must be equal opportunity for employment, development and advancement for those qualified.

We must provide competent management, and their actions must be just and ethical.

We are responsible to the communities in which we live and work and to the world community as well. We must be good citizens—support good works and charities and bear our fair share of taxes. We must encourage civic improvements and better health and education. We must maintain in good order the property we are privileged to use, protecting the environment and natural resources.

Our final responsibility is to our stockholders. Business must make a sound profit.

We must experiment with new ideas. Research must be carried on, innovative programs developed and mistakes paid for. New equipment must be purchased, new facilities provided and new products launched. Reserves must be created to provide for adverse times. When we operate according to these principles, the stockholders should realize a fair return.

Appendix D

Alignment Survey

Background to this survey:

As a people function it's vitally important that we understand the needs of the business and respond to these in a timely and appropriate manner. When we do this well we are allocating our resource and effort in the best way to achieve the business goals.

The purpose of this survey is to measure alignment within our business. We are doing this my measuring three key categories which are:

1. clarity—measures if people know what's important within the business,
2. consistency—measures of planned activities consistent with what's important and
3. commitment—measures of the business follows through by allocating resources.

This survey is **completely anonymous**. You have been sent the link to this survey having been randomly selected from a cross-section of people at your location.

Instructions:

Please answer the survey as honestly as possible. As a business we need to be absolutely clear about what is working well and what may not be working as well as it could be, so your honesty is very much appreciated! This survey has 15 questions, each of which has five possible responses.

You can also add in comments for each question where you feel you'd like to add more detail. **Please ensure you complete your survey by no later than (add your date here).**

If you have any questions about this survey the please contact (add contact details here).

Alignment Survey

For each of the following statements, please answer honestly. Your responses are confidential.

Which role best describes you?	Senior Manager	Manager	Team Leader	Specialist	Other

What is your normal work location?	Location A	Location B	Location C	Location D	Location E

Q #	Statement	Strongly agree	Agree	Don't know	Disagree	Strongly disagree
1	I know and understand the current business goals					
Comment						

2	At my location, we know what the business goals are					
Comment						
3	I think the business strategy has credibility and is realistic					
Comment						
4	At my location, we all know what the key issues are and we work together to fix them					
Comment						
5	We know that all our efforts are fully aligned with the business plan					
Comment						

Q #	Statement	Strongly agree	Agree	Don't know	Disagree	Strongly disagree
6	The business takes a long-term view of performance issues and keeps working on them until they are resolved					
Comment						
7	At my location, leaders make sure that short-term problems do not change our long-term goals					
Comment						
8	Business plans at all locations are aligned with each other and also with the overall business plan					
Comment						

9	At my location, staff at all levels are confident that we can safely deliver our business plan					
Comment						
10	At my location, leaders understand the difference between cost and value					
Comment						
11	The business uses metrics that predict future performance rather than just relying on past performance					
Comment						
12	At my location we measure our ability to deliver something before making promises in our business plan					
Comment						

13	At my location we always allocate the correct amount of resources to get the job done					
Comment						
14	At my location I know that priorities set out in the business plan will be delivered on time and budget					
Comment						
15	In the business, if something is important it will be resourced and managed correctly					
Comment						

References

Chapter one:

People Management. CIPD, April 2012

Charity Learning Consortium, Donald H Taylor, 2010

Fast Company, Why we hate HR, Keith Hammonds, 2005

Maximise Training impact by aligning learning with business goals, Jay Bahlis, 2004

Learning to change, Capita, 2010

Online survey, Learning and Skills Group, 2009

Learning and development exhibition programme, CIPD, 2012

Learning technologies conference programme, 2012

Learning technologies conference programme, 2013

TrainingZone live programme, 2012

Learning live programme, Learning and Performance Institute, 2012

The business benefits of management & leadership development, CMI/Penna, 2012

Learning and development aligning workforce with business, Aberdeen group, 2007

High impact learning cultures, Bersin & associates, 2010

Chapter two:

Life of Brian, Monty Python, 1979

Annual report, Microsoft, 2011

CEO survey, PR Week, 2006

Tough Choices or Tough Times: The Report of the New Commission on the Skills of the American Workforce, 2007

The link between management and productivity, McKinsey et al, 2006

Workforce survey, Hays, 2011

Chapter three:

The top fifty UK training companies, Pardo Fox, 2011

Learning through life, The inquiry into the future of lifelong learning, 2009

UK Employer skills survey, UK Commission for Employment and Skills, 2011

Labour market statistical bulletin, ONS, 2011

Learning and talent development survey, CIPD, 2012

General employment estimates, US department of labor, 2004

Chapter four:

Founding companies, Dow jones industrial average, 1896

Eccentric contraptions, Maurice Collins, 2004

People, planet, profit, Peter Fisk, 2010

http://www.talksport.co.uk/

www.telegraph.co.uk/

Chapter five:

Beyond Performance: How Great Organizations Build Ultimate Competitive Advantage, Keller & Price, 2011

7s Framework, McKinsey, 1982

What Really Works, Joyce, Nohria and Roberson, 2003

Chapter six:

Navigating the perfect storm in L&D, white paper, Learning and Performance Institute, 2012

Learning and Development Strategy, Bolton NHS Primary Care Trust, 2008-2010

Learning and Development Strategy, British Museum, 2007

Value propositions, www.neilrackham.com

Isaac Newton, Law of universal gravitation

The top fifty UK training companies, Pardo Fox, 2011
Value proposition, www.skillsoft.com
Value proposition, www.steria.com/uk/

Chapter seven:

First let's fire all the managers, Gary Hamel, Harvard Business
    Review, December 2011
Training Needs Analysis definition, Chartered Institute of
    Personnel and Development www.cipd.co.uk
Novartis campus Boston, www.novartis.com

Chapter eight:

Built to last: Successful habits of visionary companies, James
    Collins, 2000
Credo, Johnson & Johnson, www.jnj.com
The Leadership Challenge Project, James Kouzes and Barry
    Posner, www.leadershipchallenge.com
The One Minute Manager, Ken Blanchard, 1994
McLaren Technology Centre, www.mclaren.com
Maverick!: The Success Story Behind the World's Most Unusual
    Workplace, Ricardo Semler, 2001
Relax: A Happy Business Story by Henry Stewart, Cathy Busani
    and James Moran, 2009

Chapter nine:

Brand Failures: The Truth About the 100 Biggest Branding
    Mistakes of All Time, Matt Haig, 3 May 2011
Lean Thinking: Banish Waste and Create Wealth in Your
    Corporation, James P. Womack and Daniel T. Jones, 2003
Carbon footprint, www.guardian.co.uk

Chapter ten:

General research, Wikipedia, www.wikipedia.com

Soccernomics, Simon Kuper and Stefan Szymanski, 2012

Moneyball: The Art of Winning an Unfair Game, Michael Lewis, 2004

The Difference: How the Power of Diversity Creates Better Groups, Firms, Schools, and Societies, Scott E. Page, 2008

The 50 Most Innovative Companies 2010, businessweek, www.businessweek.com

Deals from hell: M&A Lessons That Rise Above the ashes, Robert F. Bruner, 2005

Chapter eleven:

Learning and talent development survey, CIPD, 2012

BBC Academy, www.bbctraining.com

Evaluating Training Programs: The Four Levels, Donald L. Kirkpatrick and James D. Kirkpatrick, 2006

SPIN-selling, Neil Rackham, 1995

Monty Python and the Holy Grail, 1975

European Journal of Social Psychology, Phillippa Lally and colleagues, University College London, 2009

Funky Business by Kjell Nordstrom and Jonas Ridderstrale, 1999

Return on Investment in Training and Performance Improvement Programs (Improving Human Performance), Jack J. Phillips PhD, 2003

Chapter twelve:

Aligning learning to strategic priorities, Discussion paper, Chartered Institute of Personnel and Development (CIPD), 2007

Online poll, Chartered Institute of Personnel and Development (CIPD), 2007

ABOUT THE AUTHOR

Jonathan Kettleborough has over twenty five years' experience within the People Profession combining over twenty three years' experience in computer based training, multimedia and e-learning and more than twenty years' experience in training, development and business management. Prior to establishing his own consultancy, Jonathan managed a number of training operations, ranging from internal training departments to limited companies delivering to blue chip clients. During his time in training management, Jonathan always sought to clearly align his work with the business, thereby maximising the benefits of his work. He derived much success from this approach including national and international awards and recognition. Jonathan's experience covers a wide range of industries including financial, stockbroking, IT, government, learning, telecommunications and nuclear.

Jonathan was a founder of the TenCORE user group and later engineered the merger of this group into The Association of Computer Based Training (TACT) which has since become the e-learning Network which celebrated its 25th anniversary in 2012. Jonathan was also a key member of the Northern New Media Forum and retains close ties to both the Chartered Institute of Personnel and Development and the Learning and Performance Institute where he is both a Chartered Member and Fellow.

In between his work as a business consultant, he remains active on the speaker circuit, continues to have articles published, works as external faculty to Birkbeck College and has undertaken an MBA where he gained a distinction. He is also a judge for the prestigious annual Learning Awards.

Contact details

Jonathan can be contacted via the following:

Email: jonathan@jonathankettleborough.com
LinkedIn: Jonathan Kettleborough
Twitter: @JKettleborough
Blog: www.jonathankettleborough.com

3223460R10125

Printed in Great Britain
by Amazon.co.uk, Ltd.,
Marston Gate.